OTHER BOOKS BY THIS AUTHOR:

The Doctors Guide to Starting Your Practice/Career Right

The Doctors Guide to Eliminating Debt

The Doctors Guide to Smart Career Alternatives and Retirement

The Doctors Guide to Real Estate Investing for Busy Professionals

THE
DOCTORS
GUIDE TO

Navigating a
Financial Crisis

DR. CORY S. FAWCETT

The Doctors Guide to Navigating a Financial Crisis
By Dr. Cory S. Fawcett © 2020

Scripture quotations marked NIV are taken from The Holy Bible, New International Version® NIV® Copyright © 1973 1978 1984 2011 by Biblica, Inc.™ Used by permission. All rights reserved worldwide.

Print ISBN: 978-1-61206-202-0
eBook ISBN: 978-1-61206-203-7

Interior and Cover Design by: Fusion Creative Works, FusionCW.com
Lead Editor: Jennifer Regner

For more information, visit FinancialSuccessMD.com

To purchase this book at discounted prices, go to AlohaPublishing.com or email alohapublishing@gmail.com

Published by

AlohaPublishing.com
Printed in the United States of America

Dedication

I dedicate this book to all the hardworking Americans whose income was lost or reduced during the 2020 pandemic. I hope my words help you reach a brighter tomorrow.

Signature _____ Dr. Cory S. Fawcett

Contents

Chapter 3: Stop Hemorrhaging Money 59

As a trauma surgeon, I know there's a "golden hour" right after a trauma when quick action can eliminate the urgency of the situation. Sometimes it's less than an hour, but the concept still holds—stop the bleeding, and you've got time to take care of the rest. For a financial crisis, it's more like the "golden week," when quick action on your part can make a difference. Don't let panic and fear make you miss the golden week when your actions can improve the situation and head off bigger problems.

Chapter 4: Be Aggressive at Creating Income 75

The sooner you have money coming in, the sooner your money problems will start to get better. Identify your best new job options, update your resume, and hit the streets (or web). Don't stop with the first potential bite—apply for multiple jobs at once. Depending on the cause of your crisis, the state of the job market, and especially if you don't find a job right away, look outside of your normal field. Take whatever will help you get back on your feet. If you treat your job hunt like an emergency, you will get much better results.

Chapter 5: Sell Seldom-Used Items 87

Take a look around your home and at your list of assets for things you might sell. This is the time to take a long hard look at which of those assets are really bringing you joy. If you have special collectibles, you may need to hire someone to help you sell them. Get ruthless and convert your unused or unneeded items to cash and use the cash to pay your bills. You also get the added benefit of decluttering your house.

Chapter 6: Urgent Procrastination 91

Now is the time to put off those planned vacations, that CME trip to Las Vegas, and that new car you were thinking about. If your crisis involved a crash of the stock market, that's an opportunity to do nothing, which is better than locking in losses. If you were planning to retire, you may need to postpone that retirement date. The bottom line is to put off any expenses that are not absolutely necessary.

Chapter 7: Using Your Emergency Fund 103

If you are in the midst of a financial crisis and you have not stashed away an emergency fund, the horse is already out of the barn. However if you planned ahead and have one, the most important thing is not to treat it like another paycheck. Don't dip into it just because it's easy. Continue to use it only for emergencies and look hard at whether you actually need a particular purchase. Use it to sustain a scaled-back lifestyle. Once it's gone, it's gone.

Chapter 8: Tapping Into Retirement Funds 113

Your retirement accounts are one of your financial assets, although they're not the best resource to use during an emergency. It's expensive and comes with penalties, depending on the accounts and your situation. Exhaust your other alternatives before you raid your retirement accounts. But in a true crisis, unusual times may call for unusual actions. Here is a breakdown of the rules and limitations of taking money out of retirement accounts before age 59½.

Chapter 9: Tapping Into Your Home Equity 123

If you own a home, it can be a source of money you tap into during a crisis. It's best not to think of it that way in normal circumstances—you need a place to live. Here are options and guidance for accessing your home's equity in a variety of ways. Take a look at your situation, your job prospects, where you live, your house size, your equity, and the effect of the mortgage on your ability to get by each month.

Chapter 10: Dealing With Debt 133

Debt is a thorn in your side when you have a financial crisis. Becoming familiar with the programs available to help you for each different type of loan can decrease the pain. If you owe money to a creditor and realize you won't be able to make the next payment, it's better to run toward a creditor than away from them. Let them know of your problem and give them a chance to work with you. They will give you more leeway before you've missed a payment than after.

Chapter 11: Government and Other Assistance 153

If a company as large as Chrysler needed help from the government, then you and I could certainly run into trouble that would leave us looking for their help. If a disability is the cause of your crisis, a lot of governmental programs will open up to you. Don't feel ashamed to ask for help. Government programs are designed as a safety net when trouble strikes.

Chapter 12: Friends and Family 159

Friends and family can be valuable resources during a crisis. Once your friends and family know of your problems, they can become a big support system by giving both good suggestions and monetary help. You will never know what they can do for you until you ask. But because of the long-term relationships they provide, you must be careful how you proceed. You run the risk of creating a riff in the family or losing a friendship if you handle things poorly.

Chapter 13: What Not to Do 163

Number one is don't panic. Number two is take care to keep a positive attitude—don't complain or blame. This helps no one. And number three is don't give up. Lots of people have been in your shoes. Tough times happen more than you realize and this time it is your turn to endure. Remember this is not your defining moment. Shake it off and figure out what is the next right thing for you to do and start doing it.

Chapter 14: Bankruptcy 173

Bankruptcy is a journey people take too lightly until they walk the journey themselves. It can be a big stressor with long-lasting impacts on your life and your credit score. But sometimes bankruptcy is the only way to discharge an obligation like a lease or an extreme debt when circumstances change. While it is not ideal, it is there to give people a chance to start over and there is no shame in reaching for legally prescribed options for starting over.

If you are married, a financial crisis will put great stress on your marriage. If you don't handle this carefully, you might lose your spouse. Work together on the solution to your problems, keep the communication lines open, don't place blame, and continue investing in your relationship just like you did before the financial crisis happened. Celebrate the wins. If you are aware of the stress it can create and deal with it in a proactive manner, you are likely to come out of this with your marriage stronger than ever.

You will experience the added stress of a financial crisis without a spouse to share the load, but you are not alone. Your relationships can be stressed as a result of the crisis too, and you need to keep the communication lines open with your friends and family. Stop any self-blame you are feeling. Celebrating wins is as important for single people as it is for married couples. If you have kids, involve them in discussing the crisis as much as you can. They can handle more than you think.

One of the biggest issues many professionals face is having your identity tied to your career. When your career goes, your identity is in danger of going with it. But you are not defined only by your title at work. You are also a husband/wife, father/mother, friend, son/daughter, and community member. You are still you. You still have the skills and talents you always had and the knowledge you gained in your training and experience. Other people might be interested in building on that outside the confines of your lost career.

After your income and expenses have stabilized and you are no longer in survival mode, it's time to start getting your life back to normal. Start by going back to chapter 2 and reassessing your finances again. You need to know your new starting point and what goals you want to establish—in terms of rebuilding your emergency fund, dealing with debt, and restarting contributions to retirement accounts and charities—before you can begin putting your finances back in order.

Chapter 19: Lean on Your Faith

Many people in America believe in God—however that doesn't mean there will not be hard times. Bad things happen to good people and good things happen to bad people. What's important is how you react to the bad things that happen. When you look back at this crisis, you will probably not remember all the pain, anguish, and despair you felt at the time. You are more likely to remember the good things that resulted from your temporary troubles. And most importantly, it's important to learn to find contentment no matter what your circumstances are.

Introduction

On April 23, 2020, the U.S. Department of Labor put out their weekly unemployment figures and reported more than 23,000,000 people had lost their jobs in the preceding four weeks. News channels reported food banks running out of food as thousands of cars lined up, seeking aide. Many physicians, thought to have great job security, were unable to work as elective medicine was shut down. Even in one of the richest countries in world history, people were going hungry. America was in crisis.

What happens when a crisis happens to me, and my family experiences it firsthand? Most of the time, my tragedy will not make the news. A crisis in my life, which is the most important news item of the day for me, goes unnoticed by everyone except my family.

As a surgeon, this reminds me of a saying: A minor surgery is one performed on someone else.

That's the way it is with our finances, too. It's interesting to talk about, discuss the possibilities, and ruminate over other people's financial disasters, but we really don't want to think about those possibilities happening in our own lives. Most physicians never thought this could happen to them. We might have saved and prepared for a financial crisis if we thought it could actually happen to us.

Thinking about and planning for our own catastrophes is too painful, so we often don't do it. This is the reason many people do not have a will. In order to prepare a will, we must walk through the ramifications of our own death and that is too painful.

A lot of people are in financial crisis at any given time, and often the cause is outside of their control. The crisis creates feelings of stress, fear, anger, and insecurity. There is always the possibility that life will never return to the way it was and a new normal will be established.

Sometimes events occur on a larger scale, which increases the sheer number of those in crisis. A hurricane blows through and thousands of people are suddenly homeless and jobless. A forest fire blazes a trail and the people in entire neighborhoods are left with only the clothes they were wearing when they narrowly escaped with their lives. A pandemic goes viral and millions are out of work and fearing for their lives. The stock market crashes, and retirement accounts are gutted everywhere.

You don't have to be involved in a natural disaster to face a personal financial crisis. The death of the main breadwinner in a family is a severe disaster. Being fired or laid off from a job is another. Divorce creates so many other problems on top of the economic issues. Having a stroke compounds the loss of income with enormous medical bills. Even the slow creep of overspending can lead to big financial problems.

It is important to realize that financial problems are a common occurrence. Just because we don't know of anyone in financial crisis or we don't see it in the news doesn't mean it's not happening. We tend not to tell our friends and neighbors when we are having financial difficulties because it feels like a defeat. We certainly don't want others to think we mishandled our money. But mishandling money is not usually the cause of a financial crisis.

Make no mistake, you are not alone when financial disaster strikes. Others have been where you are now. Others have come back stronger than they were before their crisis.

This moment in your life story is only one chapter of a long and incredible novel. No single chapter should ever constitute the defining moment of your life story. It is only a minor piece that shapes the sum of who you are.

Knowing this happens all the time means knowing others have won their financial battles before you. If someone else can do this, so can you.

> "That which does not kill us makes us stronger."
>
> – Friedrich Nietzsche

Crises happen often for some and rarely for others, but no one is immune. When it happens to you, turn to this book for solutions so you can find your way out. There is always a way out.

After you recover, you can better prepare for the next crisis. You might have already discovered the insufficiency of the things you did or didn't do in preparation for your current crisis. Disasters have a way of being worse than we thought they would be, leaving us underprepared.

After a message of hope, we will go through some actions you can take to get yourself out of whatever financial crisis currently haunts you. Knowledge is power and speed is the key. This book provides the knowledge you need to take back control of your destiny and rescue yourself from disaster. It will also impart on you a sense of urgency you may not have felt before. Once you are back on your feet, we will discuss ways to position yourself to be better prepared for the next financial crisis that might come your way.

Throughout the book, I will weave in my story, which starts below, as well as the stories of others who have survived their own crises to show you that others have been where you are, recovered, and lived to tell their tale. Yes, there is hope for you too.

Let's roll up our sleeves and get to work resolving your crisis. You've got this!

MY STORY PART 1: THE GOOD LIFE

In the summer of 1992, life was good as I started the final year of my general surgery residency. This was the home stretch on a very long journey to reach my dream career. Four years of premed at Stanford University, four years of medical school at Oregon Health and Science University, and now I was in my fifth year of residency at Kern Medical Center in Bakersfield, California.

It was the fourth year of marriage for Carolyn and me, and we were living the American dream. Our three-bedroom, 1,500-square-foot apartment with an attached two-car garage was very comfortable. Both of the cars sitting in our garage were paid off, fairly new, and in good condition. Our only debt was the last $6,000 of my student loans. Brian, our first child, was a healthy 4-month-old who was finally sleeping through the night. Our retirement funds were growing, and we were saving for the down payment on our first house after residency. As two decades of dreaming and hard work were coming to an end with this final year of training, it was time to find a job that would allow us to spend the rest of our lives in wedded bliss.

My wife's family lived in Portland, Oregon, and my family lived four hours south in Medford. We decided our future would lie somewhere on Interstate 5, between our two families. In the late fall of that year, I set out to find a general surgery practice to support our growing family on the Interstate 5 corridor.

Over the next few months, I explored some possible practices. After narrowing the choice to two, we set up a formal interview with each of them. Carolyn and I made a trip to meet the partners and their families, tour their medical offices and hospitals, and explore the towns. After choosing the practice that best suited us, we began contract negotiations.

This was such an exciting time for us. In March, just three months before graduating, my signature was inked on the final contract and it was mailed off for their signatures. I couldn't have been happier. My new job was located almost exactly between our two families.

Then disaster struck, throwing all our plans out the window.

Chapter 1

THERE IS ALWAYS HOPE!

TIME HEALS ALL WOUNDS

Your life might have been running along like mine was, exactly as it should. But we must remember that nobody's life runs on track all the time. Whatever crisis you are experiencing at this time will pass and you will heal. It is part of the life cycle of a disaster. Take, for instance, the following three natural disasters my wife and I have toured at various stages of recovery. I discuss them not in the order we encountered them, but based on the stage of their recovery, with the earliest recovery stage presented first.

The November 2018 forest fire nearly destroyed the town of Paradise, California. We drove through the area five months after the fire. Entire neighborhoods were wiped out and became only a sea of foundations covered with rubble and ash. Each one of those foundations marked a devastated family who had lost everything.

We were traveling in our motorhome and had planned to stop for the night, but there wasn't a single RV site for miles. Every campground was filled with displaced families living in trailers provided by the Federal Emergency Management Agency (FEMA). Paradise was still grieving their loss and doing their initial clean up.

We toured another disaster in the middle stage of recovery, 10 years after the event. The lower ninth ward in New Orleans was wiped out by Hurricane Katrina in 2005. This area had flooded and remained under water for months. We found New Orleans residents were living in the area again. Some houses had been rebuilt and some still stood empty with high-water marks near the second-story roof line. There was still recovery to be done, but the signs of life had returned.

On our third disaster tour, in Halifax, Nova Scotia, the people had completely recovered. Standing on top of the walls of the Halifax Citadel National Historic Site, which sits on a hill overlooking this beautiful city, no signs of a prior disaster could be seen.

In December 1917, a ship carrying explosives collided with another ship in the harbor and caught on fire. The fire led to what was at the time the largest manmade explosion in history. The waterfront area for half a mile inland was turned into rubble and sticks. Thousands died and even more were left homeless. Yet during our visit, I couldn't see any evidence of the disaster and wouldn't have known it had ever happened if I had not gone to the Maritime Museum of the Atlantic and seen the pictures.

These three disasters, at various recovery stages, illustrate the healing power of time. Healing happens in stages. First, you must get through the immediate crisis. Then, you assess the damage. Finally, you recover and rebuild, making things better than they were before and able to withstand future disasters.

It's like the opening segment of the 70s show, *The Six Million Dollar Man.* Every show started with footage of Steve Austin's airplane crash and stated, "We can rebuild him. We have the technology. We can make him better than he was before; better, stronger, faster."

That is the pattern for how your financial crisis will evolve. At first you will be devastated and not know what to do. Then you will figure out what you need to do and begin to repair the damage. You will eventually fully recover and be stronger because of the journey. Finally, you will make a plan to avoid going down that road again.

ATTITUDE MAKES THE DIFFERENCE

In the *Batman* TV series from the late 60s, Batman would find himself captured by his nemesis in almost every episode. When the nemesis was sure their contraption would do away with the caped crusader, they would leave Batman and Robin to die alone. But without fail, Batman had something in his utility belt, which I always thought of as his Batbelt, that could solve the problem. Treat this book like your own personal Batbelt.

I realize fictional characters do not represent real life situations and their outcomes are scripted, but they do give us a relatable example of how we should approach our problems. Batman represents what we all need to do when a crisis hits. **He does not panic**—instead, he puts time and effort into calmly finding a solution to his problems, and there is always a solution.

The same is true for you. There is always a solution. The sun will rise tomorrow and in 10 years, what appeared to be a financial disaster will not seem as bad as it did when you experienced it. As long as you can find a way to keep a roof over your head and food in your belly, you will survive. Everything else is gravy.

Don't try to do this alone. Get help. Ask friends and family what they would do. Involve your spouse and kids. They are in this with you, so let them be part of the solution.

Regarding hope, what matters most is your attitude. If you don't think there is any hope, you are right. If you believe there is hope, you are also right, and your outcome will be better.

THERE IS ALWAYS HOPE!

I love this poem written more than 100 years ago by Walter D. Wintle. Over the years it has been published in several slightly different versions and is found under two different titles: *Thinking* and *The Man Who Thinks He Can*. Here is the version Wikipedia claims is likely the original:

> If you think you are beaten, you are;
> If you think you dare not, you don't.
> If you'd like to win, but you think you can't,
> It is almost a cinch you won't.
>
> If you think you'll lose, you've lost;
> For out in this world we find
> Success begins with a person's will
> It's all in the state of mind.
>
> If you think you're outclassed, you are;
> You've got to think high to rise.
> You've got to be sure of yourself before
> You can ever win the prize.
>
> Life's battles don't always go
> To the stronger or faster man;
> But sooner or later the person who wins
> Is the one who thinks he can!

You need this can-do attitude if you want to conquer your crisis. While facing your financial problem, only you can decide which of Winnie-the-Pooh's friends you will act like: Tigger or Eeyore.

Eeyore is very down on everything. "Poor me, I can't get anything right. Nothing good ever happens to me. I'll never win."

But Tigger—he is a very different animal. Tiggers are fun, fun, fun, fun, fun. It doesn't matter what Tigger faces; he will find the fun in it. You need to choose to be a Tigger, even in the worst of situations. Attitude is everything.

Yes, I know it's hard to be Tigger in the midst of a crisis. It's hard for Batman when he is tied up and hanging over a boiling vat of oil with a candle burning the rope that holds him up. While Robin is yelling, "Holy burning rope, Batman!" Batman is busy figuring out a way to get out of this mess. Robin can't figure it out because he is spending too much time reacting and worrying. Batman is spending his time thinking. And he finds the answer.

These fictional characters are fun to talk about, but there are also real-life examples of digging out of disaster that we can look to.

Abraham Lincoln was a country lawyer who became president and led the nation through its biggest crisis, the Civil War. Over 1,000,000 Americans died or were injured in that war.

Lincoln did not survive the war, but the nation he led came back stronger.

Nelson Mandela was serving a life sentence in prison. He was released after 27 years and later became president of South Africa.

George Washington and his troops were in the depths of despair when they wintered in Valley Forge. No supplies and no shelter made for a difficult winter and cost 2,000 people their lives. He and the army came back from this low point to win the Revolutionary War.

Helen Keller was deaf and blind, yet she overcame. Learning to communicate, she eventually earned a bachelor's degree and became a political activist, author, and lecturer.

Franklin D. Roosevelt led the country through the Great Depression and World War II. Both were tough times for our country, but we made it through.

No matter what situation you find yourself dealing with right now, you can overcome it, just like many who have been there before you. Put your mind to the problem and never give up hope.

When you think you've thought
of everything, you haven't.
So keep thinking.

MY STORY PART 2: THE DISASTER

After I sent off the signed contract for my great new job, I waited for them to send me the fully signed copy. I waited and waited and waited. During the first week of April, after what seemed like an excessive amount of time for them to sign the contract, I gave my future senior partner a call.

The conversation was not what I expected. Apparently I was not the only candidate they had been negotiating a contract with. While I was under the assumption I would be their future partner, unbeknownst to me, they were also looking at another surgeon. My future partner told me they decided to hire the other guy. Then he said he was sorry.

My world came crashing down.

At that point, graduation was less than three months away and I didn't have a job. It was now the wrong time of year to look for a medical position. By that point, all the graduating residents had found jobs and the recent openings were filled.

I contacted the other practice where I interviewed, and the position was already filled. There were no longer any general surgery job openings in our dream location. I was three months from being a highly educated, fully trained, unemployed surgeon.

This was a moment of great despair for me. It was a disaster! Everything up until this point in my life had gone exactly according to my plan. Now, for the first time in my life, I didn't know what to do. I didn't have a plan for this. Everyone at Carolyn's office knew she would be leaving her job and moving when my residency was complete in less than three months. Both of us would be out of work and we would have no income.

How would I provide for my family? How would we eat? Where would we live? What would we do? I was distressed and depressed.

That was when my wife suggested maybe things weren't as bad as they seemed. Maybe there was still hope.

Chapter 2

ASSESS THE SITUATION

FACE THE FEAR

So you find yourself in the midst of a financial crisis. Something has happened to tip the scales against you, financially, and now you don't know what to do. The unknown is scary. Many people fail to act because of their fear of the unknown or of doing the wrong thing.

In 1933 when Franklin D. Roosevelt gave his first inaugural speech during the Great Depression, he said this:

"So first of all let me assert my firm belief that the only thing we have to fear is fear itself – nameless, unreasoning, unjustified terror, which paralyzes needed efforts to convert retreat into advance."

He wanted people to realize their fear—their emotional response—was stopping them from advancing, not the underlying problems causing the fear. If we can conquer fear, we can get on with solving the problem.

The first thing to consider about your fear is the likelihood that you are blowing the problem out of proportion. This could start a downward spiral of negative thinking when in fact you don't know what the outcome will be.

Most of the time, things are not nearly as bad as we imagine them to be. Imagine having a leg amputated, which would be very bad—but it could have been both legs, which would be worse. You can still do a lot with one leg. Many people live a normal life with one leg. It is not the end of the world.

During a crisis, we often become hyper-focused on what we lost, allowing its effect to grow bigger and bigger. Get a handle on the true severity of the problem. Most of the time, it is not as bad as you think. Even if it is as bad as you think, there are ways to deal with every crisis. Don't get so focused on the loss that you forget about what you still have.

Is there a roof over your head? Check.

Is there food in the cupboards? Check.

Is there gas in the car? Check.

Does your phone work? Check.

Are you and your loved ones safe and uninjured? Check.

If you are healthy and sheltered, and have food, communication, and transportation, then you have all the tools you need to deal with the crisis. If you don't have at least these tools, there may be ways to connect with others to get them.

Another favorite TV show of mine was *MacGyver,* which aired in the mid-1980s and was rebooted in 2016. No matter what situation MacGyver found himself in, he considered the resources he had available and found a solution to his problem. He was so good at doing this his name came to mean solving a problem with what you have on hand, like one would "MacGyver" a solution. *(I heard this reference used in a news broadcast the day I wrote this.)*

Just like MacGyver, you need to take a look around and assess the situation—without panic, without fear. Use your head and assess the resources you have on hand to fight for a resolution to your crisis.

When MacGyver has duct tape, superglue, bubblegum, and a Swiss Army knife, he has all he needs to break out of Fort Knox. Mostly what he has is his ability to think and reason and work out a solution.

My wife and I recently watched the movie *Frozen II*. At a moment when Anna is in great despair over the loss of her sister and her friend, she sings a song with the following phrase:

You must go on and do the next right thing.

What a great concept. You don't need to conquer your fears. You don't need to have all your ducks in a row. You don't need all the answers. You only need to do the next right thing. Take the next step. Move forward and you will be one step closer to your destination. No, you will not be there yet, but you will be one step closer to victory.

When Carolyn and I walked 450 miles on the Camino de Santiago in Spain during the summer of 2019, it seemed like the end was so far away, and it was—450 miles is a long walk. But we didn't need to walk 450 miles. We only needed to walk to the next town, which might be two miles.

My body was hurting, but I knew I could make it to the next town. I was not so sure about making it to Santiago, but I knew others had done it before me. So, I did the next right thing and walked to the next town. And then the next town. And then the next town. It wasn't very long before the next town was Santiago and we completed the journey.

It's time for you to do the next right thing. It's time to conquer the fear of the unknown and make it known. You might still be scared and feel defeated, but you will be on the journey to recovery. You've got this.

In order to assess the situation, the next right step is to make a list of all your assets. The list below should help jog your memory of what assets you might have.

LIST YOUR FINANCIAL ASSETS

BANK ACCOUNTS

Start by listing all your bank accounts. Do you have more than one? Sometimes when you find yourself in a bad financial situation, it's good to pool your money. Many bank accounts require a minimum balance to avoid charges. If you have four bank accounts and each has a $1,000 minimum balance, then you are tying up $4,000 to avoid charges. You sure don't need extra bank charges right now.

Close three of the accounts and move all the money into one account. You will then have a lump sum of $4,000 with only a $1,000 required minimum bank balance. Then if the balance falls too low, you will only get charged for one account.

Seeing all the money in one place is also psychologically helpful. It makes you feel like you have more. Seeing one $4,000 account feels better than seeing a $1,000 balance, even though you know there are four of them.

NON-RETIREMENT BROKERAGE ACCOUNTS

You might own stock, bonds, and mutual funds in a standard brokerage account. These accounts don't have any special rules like a retirement account might have. The great thing about these investments is they are readily available to use with no questions, penalties, or forms to fill out. The money is yours to spend however you see fit.

Don't forget about tax loss harvesting. If the stock market has dropped, you can sell a stock or mutual fund at a loss, up to $3,000, and buy a similar replacement in your account. Essentially your account remains the same, but now you can take a $3,000 tax deduction. Every little bit helps.

RETIREMENT ACCOUNTS

Do you know how much you have in your retirement accounts? Most people don't know. The money in most retirement accounts gets put there through direct deposit from a payroll deduction they never see. Now would be a good time to see what the total is in the account.

Check your last statement and add this account and its balance to your list. Then check the statements for all of your retirement accounts. I have five different retirement accounts to include on my list:

- ✓ 401(k) from my medical practice
- ✓ Rollover IRA for me
- ✓ Traditional IRA for me
- ✓ Traditional IRA for my wife
- ✓ 403(b) from my residency

Don't try to do the math in your head. Get a grand total of all the retirement accounts. Don't use your best guess. Get the actual value. You should be able to check it online, look at your last statement, or contact the retirement specialist for your company to get the current total.

HEALTH SAVINGS ACCOUNT (HSA)

Like the retirement accounts, you likely don't know how much is in this account. Check your last statement and add it and its current balance to your financial assets list.

PROPERTY

Do you own any property? This includes the house you may be living in. If so, do you know what it's worth? Most people have no idea what their property is worth. You can look at your last property tax statement to get the real market value of the property, which is only an estimate. The more time that has transpired since you purchased the property, the further off the estimate might be.

You can ask a Realtor to look at your property to give you an estimate of its likely sales price in the current market. If your financial crisis is caused by a widespread event, like if the plant that employs 45% of the people in town just closed, the value of property might be uncertain. In a steady-state environment, a Realtor can make a pretty good estimate of a property's value. But in a volatile market, that estimate becomes fuzzy.

DETERMINE THE EQUITY IN YOUR HOME OR OTHER PROPERTY

Once you know the value of a property, subtract the remaining balance on your property loan to get the amount of equity you currently have in that property. You might need to ask your lender for your current loan balance. If you don't have a loan against the property, then its current value is your equity. Put the equity of your property on your financial assets list.

BUSINESS VALUE

If you own a business, it has a value. As long as it was not the cause of the crisis, you should be able to estimate its worth.

You might also have some deferred income sitting in the business. When I was a partner in my medical practice, our pay was based on our production. Since our workload varied throughout the year, each surgeon was paid a consistent monthly income equivalent to substantially less than one-twelfth of their expected annual income. This allowed money to accumulate in the business account throughout the year. Whatever was left in the business at the end of the year was distributed based on what we each had actually earned.

That meant throughout each year, the business bank account was growing and a portion of that money would be distributed to me at the end of the year. That money might be available in an emergency.

ACCOUNTS RECEIVABLE

If you have a business that bills customers, like a doctor's office, then you have a lag time between when bills are sent and when the payments are received. This amount of uncollected money is your accounts receivable.

This money will still be coming in even if you are no longer working.

UNSOLD INVENTORY

If you have a business that sells goods, then you might have goods in inventory or in a warehouse waiting to be sold. Count the number and value of these products. One way to gain some cash is to sell down the inventory without replacing it. I sell books, for instance. If I sell a book out of my stock and don't replace it immediately, my income increases in the short term.

EMERGENCY FUND

If you have been preparing for a future crisis, then you should have a nice emergency fund—preferably with six months of your living expenses tucked away. But if you are like most Americans, you don't even have $1,000 saved for an emergency.

Whatever your emergency fund looks like, find its balance and write it on your financial assets list. If you have been dipping into it for nonemergencies like buying a car or for the down payment on a house, then the balance might be less than you think.

PERSONAL LOANS

If you have loaned money to family or friends, now is the time to ask if they could repay the loan. You lent money to them in their time of need, and now you are in need. Having the money returned, or even a portion of the money, would be helpful.

Often this will be met with, "But I don't have it right now." After all, there's a reason they needed you to lend them the money in the first place. But you will not get it if you do not ask.

CASH VALUE LIFE INSURANCE

If you have life insurance with a cash value, contact your insurance agent and find out the details.

There are two values you want to know. The first option is cashing out the policy. How much money would you get if you terminated the life insurance policy today? This is the money the insurance company has invested for you from your monthly payments.

The second option is to take out a loan against the balance of your cash value account. This was one of the "great" benefits the agent told you about when they sold you the policy. You can borrow your own money and pay yourself back the amount of the loan plus interest. You can get this money without taxes or penalties, but you do need to pay it back. If you were to die before the loan is paid back, the proceeds of the policy will be used to pay back the remaining loan balance before being distributed to your heirs. Find out how much you can borrow.

CERTIFICATES OF DEPOSIT

Take a look at any CDs (certificates of deposit) you might have. You want to know the current value, the maturity date, and any penalty you would pay if you cashed it in early.

ANNUITIES

Each annuity is different, so you will need to contact the company holding the annuity, tell them your situation, and let them know you're considering cashing out the annuity. Ask them what the consequences will be and what the cash-out value is.

GOVERNMENT BILLS, NOTES, AND BONDS

There are several types of government bonds available, each with a different set of rules. If you have government bonds, find out what their value would be if you redeemed them early. There might be penalties or taxes owed. If you are in an area that has been declared a disaster, then the penalty rules for early redemption might be reduced or removed.

Older bonds were issued in paper while the new bonds, those issued after January 1, 2012, are electronic.

GOLD OR SILVER STASHES

Some people believe gold and silver will be a saving grace in the event of a national or worldwide financial meltdown. Every time the stock market falls, gold and silver ads appear on TV. If you have stashed away some precious metal, figure out how much you have and what it would be worth if you sold it. Using it in your current situation might be exactly why you bought it in the first place.

COIN COLLECTIONS

Collectable coins do not sell for their face value. A rare silver dollar will sell for much more than a dollar. If you have been collecting coins, get an estimate of the current value of your collection. There may be special pieces in your collection that can be sold individually.

Do not spend collectable coins as if they were money. We have coin-operated laundry facilities at our apartment buildings.

Now and then we have found a big run of silver quarters in the machines. Obviously, someone used an old quarter collection to do their laundry. I don't think they knew that each silver quarter they put in the machine was worth $7. We now have that silver quarter collection.

COLLECTABLE ART

If you have been an art collector, you might have several pieces of value in your house. The actual value of a piece of art is hard to determine and depends on its condition. It may be hard to sell as well, but check to see what you have. Don't forget to check the painting you inherited when your grandmother passed away. She might have purchased an original that is now valuable and you didn't know it.

OTHER COLLECTABLES

People collect many things: baseball cards, Depression glass, dolls, game-playing cards, antiques, comic books, classic cars, stamps, wine, books, toys, Avon cologne bottles, motorcycles, cigarette lighters, furniture, autographs, magazines, fine china, spoons, figurines, music boxes, perfume bottles, silverware, lunch boxes, teapots, beer steins, movie posters, campaign buttons, records, musical instruments, souvenirs, model cars, and so much more.

If you have a collection of any kind, get it appraised. A nice antique tea set may be worth a lot more to you as this month's mortgage payment than it was as something pretty to look at on the shelf.

JEWELRY

I didn't realize the total value of the jewelry I had given to my wife over the years until it was all stolen. When I added up what I had spent on each piece for the insurance company, I had a rude awakening.

You may have some nice pieces of jewelry that can be sold and replaced with an inexpensive alternative. Although jewelry is hard to value yourself, a quick trip to a jeweler will give you a good idea of what your jewels are worth. You can sell some pieces at local jewelry stores, pawnshops, worthy.com, eBay, Craigslist, and more.

SPARE ROOM

If you live in a house that is larger than you need, that space becomes a valuable asset. You could take in a long-term renter or use it as an Airbnb for short-term dwellers.

During my fourth year of medical school, I lived in a man's house who had divorced and needed some extra money. I rented the basement and I suspect he used the rent money to make his mortgage payment.

CREDIT CARD PERKS

Don't forget about those points you've accumulated on your credit card. They can be used to purchase things you need, so check out what options you have to use them. A free airplane flight for an interview would be a big help right now.

If you have any other financial assets in addition to these, add them to the list.

LIST YOUR SKILLS

Most people only see their own monetary value based on their current job. I am a surgeon, so for me, the best use of my skills is as a surgeon. Other skills I have that might be in demand are often forgotten as they are so overshadowed by the marketability of my surgical skills.

But what happens when I can't be a surgeon anymore? I could have lost my license or my ability to operate, such as if I were unable to stand for several hours.

The main skill you use as a profession is not your only skill. I wrote a book about alternative career options for doctors called *The*

Doctors Guide to Smart Career Alternatives and Retirement. Turns out even the skill of being a surgeon can be used in other ways.

Society has moved into a "side hustle" or "gig" economy era. People are using skills such as driving to earn extra money by being an Uber driver, for instance. There are alternative ways to use your many skills to generate income. You might not realize how many marketable skills you have.

My son, Keith, is a whiz at operating a computer. His friends and relatives, like me, are constantly asking him how to fix something on their computer or phone. He doesn't realize his skill is marketable. Since it's easy for him, he thinks it's easy for everyone and therefore it's not something with which he could make a living. But his skill could easily become a business. He could advertise that he could help with your computer or phone problems, and people would buy his services. Sometimes we don't see a way to monetize the things we are most familiar with.

If your skills can be used online, which means you can do the job from home, then you can post your services on sites like Upwork, Hubstaff Talent, Credo, and Fiver.

Make a list of your skills that others might pay for. Following are some ideas to help get you started. Think outside the box here.

COMPUTER SKILLS

Computer skills are in great demand today. Banking is online, communications are online, smartphones are everywhere, and lots of people are building websites. Many people need help getting started.

If you are particularly good with computers, there are a lot of people who will pay you to help them—especially people in older generations who did not grow up with computers or smartphones.

MUSICAL ABILITY

Everyone seems to want to play a musical instrument. If you already can play one, then you can teach others to play as well.

I play several instruments and when I perform in public, I am often asked if I give lessons. I do not. But if I needed some money because of a financial crisis, I would be happy to give music lessons. I suspect I could teach music full time if I needed the income.

WRITING

With most of commerce moving online, there's a great need for writers. Every website needs people to write articles and create content. If you can write a publishable article or design an advertisement, you could be a big asset to someone's team.

You can also do freelance writing for magazines and news outlets. Every time you get a pamphlet, someone wrote it. Editors and proofreaders are also needed for the plethora of self-published books popping up as well as for online publications and marketing materials.

TUTORING STUDENTS

Getting kids into college is a big deal. Many wealthy parents go to great lengths to get their children into big-name colleges. Some are even going to jail for bending the rules. If parents will go to that much trouble, there is a market to help college-bound kids improve their grades in a time-honored and legal way.

Many of us have a subject we excelled at in school. If you have one of these, then you can tutor high school students in that subject. When college-bound kids are struggling with one subject, many parents will pay to give them a boost. That's where you come in.

PAINTING

Everyone thinks they can paint. But if you actually paint well, there are many painting jobs you can fill without first spending lots of money on ladders, scaffolding, or equipment to get started. There's always a demand for people with the ability to paint rooms, fences, back porches, and even stain or paint furniture or cabinets. Since paint doesn't last long, painting jobs can always be found.

CONSTRUCTION

Building is a constant activity. If you have any skills in the construction field, there is a need for you.

HANDYMAN

There are many people who don't know how to fix things. In our throwaway society, we are losing the ability to do even the easiest repairs. If you can do small repairs, you will be in demand. TaskRabbit and Nextdoor are good ways to get your name and skills out to the public.

There are older people living in their own homes who can no longer do simple repair and maintenance jobs around their house. They need a handyman who can clean gutters, replace light bulbs in high light fixtures, or fix a broken doorknob.

LEADERSHIP

If you have been a manager or worked in any other leadership capacity, those skills translate into every field of work.

SALES

Not everyone is a born salesperson. In fact, no one is because selling is a learned skill. Some people pick it up more quickly than others. A vast variety of things are sold through salespeople, including cars, clothes, houses, motorhomes, boats . . . pick a product you are already knowledgeable about and start there. I have owned three motorhomes over the last 26 years. During the walk-through of my last motorhome purchase, I knew more about the new motorhome than the salesman who was helping me. Because of my experience, I could have easily done his job.

FITNESS

Obesity is a major problem today. Thus, people have gotten into a fitness craze to fight it off. If you have skills in this area, you can help people with their personal fitness. Think outside the box and go to people to help them where they are.

Some people would like to play their sport better. If you are good at a particular sport, you can train others as their personal coach.

Nutritional coaching is big today, as well as wellness coaching. If you have this special interest, you have a ready-made market waiting for you.

VIDEOGRAPHY

This is a skill that more and more people need. YouTube, Facebook, Instagram, TikTok, and others are being flooded with videos. But not everyone who wants to post a video knows how to accomplish it. You can either teach them how or post their videos for them.

PHOTOGRAPHY

Smartphones now have such good cameras that everyone is getting into photography. But the results aren't always good. Teaching people how to take good pictures is a marketable skill. Taking the pictures for them is also a good way to make an income.

PEOPLE SKILLS

Friendly people are needed to work in areas that have contact with the public. I had a receptionist who was such a joy to be around. She always had a smile and something good to say. Ten seconds around her and your day became brighter. If this is you, you are needed wherever people interface with a business.

DRIVING

The gig economy has really helped those who like to drive. Moving people for money has become easy with companies like Uber and Lyft. Other companies like UPS and Federal Express need delivery workers, and even hospitals need couriers to take specimens and intercompany mail to labs and departments at their other locations. There's also a whole group of special transport companies, like medical transport, which deliver people to their doctor's or physical therapist's office. During the pandemic shutdown, many restaurants that had never offered takeout were hiring delivery drivers.

CONSULTING

If you were good at a prior occupation, you can teach others to be more proficient at it. There's a whole group of people online who want to teach you something. I became a financial coach for doctors. When I put my profile on LinkedIn, I got many requests to link with people who consult with consultants to help them find clients. Even consultants have consultants.

ONLINE SALES

Garage sales are being replaced by platforms like Craigslist, eBay, and Facebook Marketplace. I had a friend who was moving to a new town and didn't want to go through the hassle of a garage sale, but he had many things he wanted to sell. He was not familiar with selling online, so he hired someone to price and sell his treasures for him. They split the proceeds of the sales, which netted him more than having a garage sale. If you know how to sell online, there is a need to fill.

GARDENING

Do you like working in the yard? Many people don't. I have a gardener who comes once a week to take care of my yard. He doesn't do much more than chop and blow. But at least I don't have to do it.

PET CARE

If you are good with animals, consider offering your services as a dog walker, trainer, or pet sitter. Cats, snakes, birds, and exotic animals need care too. Their sitters may come at a premium because of special skills.

LOCAL KNOWLEDGE

Do you live in a place where lots of tourists visit? Did you grow up there? Do you know all the old stories? Are you friends with business owners or museum owners whose places tourists would like to visit? Is there significant history in your area, like the Civil War, that you would like to learn more about and share your newfound knowledge with others? Do you love to tell stories? These are great prerequisites for a tour guide. You can freelance or become employed with a tour company. Some towns may require you to be registered.

BARTERING

Keep in mind that all these skills can be used to barter for things you need. "I'll repair your fence if you'll watch my kids two mornings a week for the next month." Get creative.

LIST YOUR CONNECTIONS OR "PEOPLE ASSETS"

Connections are a huge benefit in a crisis. I was an assistant coach for my father's Babe Ruth baseball team during college and I needed a job. One of the kids on the team was the son of a prominent businessman in town who had a lot of employees. I approached him after a game and asked how I could go about getting a job with his company. He told me what to do and I followed his instructions and got hired. I later learned he asked the personnel department to find a job for me if I showed up to apply.

Who do you know in the community with great hiring pull?

Who among your friends and relatives might be able to help you out with their connections?

Do you have a relative you could move in with for a time? When I first went to medical school, I lived in the basement of a relative's house for the first few months, until I found a roommate close to school.

Do you know someone who is well off who might loan you money in a pinch?

Do you have a friend who might want to be your roommate? They could move in with you, you could move in with them, or you could both get a new place together.

Write down everyone you can think of who may be able to further your reach in attaining employment or support.

BE SURE OF YOUR INSURANCE ASSETS

Sometimes we forget things when we're in the middle of a crisis. We often have several types of insurance to cover several types of issues. Car accidents, floods, tornados, hurricanes, earthquakes, accidental death and dismemberment, trip cancellations, extended warrantees, etc.

Jog your memory as to what types of insurance you have and which ones might come into play in your current situation.

I recently had a person drive their car into the side of one of my apartment buildings. The unit was condemned and needed expensive repairs. I expected the auto insurance of the driver to cover the damages.

The contractor doing the repairs suggested I contact my own insurance company about the issue. My insurance on the building offered better coverage than the driver's auto insurance. It also covered lost rent while the tenant was out of the unit. Between the two insurance companies, all the repairs were paid in full.

If your crisis was caused by a disability, it's time to read your disability policy. What does it cover? How much money will they pay? What is the waiting period before you can start collecting money?

Now that you have assessed the situation by reviewing your assets, you have a good grasp of where to start on this journey out of your crisis. In the next chapter, it will be time to take action.

MY STORY PART 3: THE ASSESSMENT

While I was having a pity party about the freight train of unemployment headed my way, my wife decided to flex her superpowers and save the day. She pointed out we still had options. This was not the end of the world. It could not possibly be as bad as I was thinking. The imagined pain of an upcoming problem is much worse than the actual pain.

She pointed out some things I had not thought about. Did I really want to become partners in a group that would do what that employer did to me? Maybe it was good I didn't get the job. There might be trouble there we didn't know about. Even though I was devastated by what happened, it might be for the better in the long run.

She hadn't given official notice at her job yet, so she could stay on and continue to earn an income. Yes, it was true my job would come to an end soon, but with her working, we would take a 50% pay cut, not a 100% pay cut.

In the meantime, I should begin a new job search. The area where we wanted to live contained enough cities that there was bound to be another general surgery practice looking for a partner. Maybe there was a job that hadn't been advertised yet.

We hadn't given our 30 days' notice for our apartment, so we could stay until I found a job. A few years ago, I was excited because I could get paid to moonlight in the emergency department, so why couldn't I do some moonlighting if the job search went long?

She pointed out I would eventually find a job. After all, the next year's residents would need to find jobs, so there would be lots of openings over the next few months. We were also healthy and had a little money in the bank. We could get through this.

She was right. The world was not coming to an end, and we had options. We prayed we would find the perfect practice, and I set out to make a new plan.

Chapter 3

STOP HEMORRHAGING MONEY

IT'S TIME FOR ACTION

When faced with a financial crisis, it's important to act quickly. If you follow the news in every natural disaster, the responding agency is always criticized for not acting quickly enough. No matter how fast they were, it wasn't fast enough.

That's because speed is your friend in a disaster. You can't sit and wait for someone to come and save you. You must act quickly to save yourself or to save others.

I spent 23 years as a trauma surgeon. There is a "golden hour" in trauma—the first 60 minutes after an injury. The trauma team has less than 60 minutes to address the problem or the chance the patient will die climbs rapidly.

In reality, you don't have 60 minutes for every kind of trauma. If the airway is cut off, you only have about four minutes. But the concept that speed is important still holds true. You have a limited time, right after the accident, to get the best benefit from your actions—the golden hour.

I have encountered many trauma victims who needed a single quick action to eliminate the urgency of their condition. Once the emergency was addressed, we could slow down and work on the rest of the issues.

A good example of this is a cut to the forearm that severs an artery. The victim immediately puts pressure on the artery to stop the bleeding and calls 911. The paramedics continue to apply pressure on the artery to stop the bleeding, while putting the patient in the ambulance and heading to the hospital with their lights and siren on. They arrive in the emergency department with blood all over the place from the bleeding artery. The lost blood cannot be reclaimed and used to keep the victim alive.

I can quickly put a clamp on the bleeding artery and the emergency is over. The patient is no longer at risk of bleeding to death. Now we have time to alert the needed staff, get the operating room ready, and repair the artery. Had the victim not used pressure to stop the bleeding immediately while waiting for help to arrive, they would have bled to death before reaching the hospital. The sooner the bleeding is stopped, the more blood remains in the bloodstream for their heart to use to keep their body functioning.

You need to treat your financial crisis with the same urgency as a trauma victim who might bleed to death. Think in terms of the "golden week."

THE GOLDEN WEEK

Right at the start of the crisis, you need to stop the hemorrhage. In a financial crisis, your expenses are in effect hemorrhaging money. Stopping the money from hemorrhaging means to **stop spending money**. You must keep the money in the bank and use what you have only for necessities. The sooner you stop the hemorrhage of money, the more money you will have to keep you alive and well. Treat your money with the same intense desire to conserve it as if you were saving your own blood. Think in terms of scaling back your lifestyle.

So why don't people tend to jump right in and stop the money hemorrhage? Because we like the things money has been doing for us and we don't want them to stop. We want to maintain our current lifestyle. We hope something will miraculously fix this problem and we won't be forced to make the hard cuts that might hurt. We are waiting for the ambulance to arrive so they can fix it.

I once consulted on a sick patient with a dead and infected leg. I knew there was no way to save that leg and if we did not amputate it right away, the patient would likely be dead in the next

48 hours from the infection. But the patient would not give his consent to amputate the leg. Although there was no way to save the leg and keeping the leg meant dying, he would not consent to losing his leg. He had previously decided he never wanted to have his leg amputated, and now stuck with his prior reasoning—he would rather die than have his leg removed.

I have coached people who are in the beginning of a financial crisis. I can see that if they don't make some big cuts in their spending right away, they will soon not have any money left to work with.

I might suggest they pull their children out of private school, saving $2,000 a month. But they previously decided private school was a necessity, and they're stuck in their prior reasoning. Their children's education is a priority and they won't consent to the amputation of the private school, even though there is a viable free option available.

In these cases, they often stay with the private school until their money actually runs out. When there is no money left to pay the tuition, then their children switch to public school. Because of the delay, they now have several thousand dollars less to use to get through their financial crisis.

Is there really any overall gain by delaying the inevitable cuts? No! The inevitable will happen and the hard cuts need to be made at the onset of the financial crisis.

Your best chance of survival is to make the cuts during the golden week and preserve all the cash you can to keep your household running.

Delaying this decision by trying to hold onto "normal" will only make the situation worse. A crisis calls for hard decisions. Some new and creative thinking is necessary. You need to become MacGyver.

I watched the news as the 2020 pandemic devastated New York City. Some hospitals were discussing putting two patients on one ventilator. This would never be done in normal times. But these were not normal times. If the hospital is out of ventilators and one more patient needed one to stay alive, something has to give.

In that crisis moment they had three choices:

1. Let the new patient die.
2. Take the ventilator from a patient who is likely to die and give it to the new patient while letting the first patient die.
3. Have two patients share one ventilator.

I listened to doctors in another part of the country explain to the New York doctors why they should never put two patients on one ventilator. Of course, the doctors giving the advice were not facing the same crisis the New York doctors were facing.

During a crisis, options have to be considered that would not be chosen in a normal situation. If you are out of ventilators and more patients are pouring in, you need to get creative and you may need to do something not normally done—and you need to do it right now!

Treat your financial crisis with the same urgency. You will need to make decisions you would not make under normal circumstances. But these are not normal circumstances. The time to cut spending is before you run out of money—because if that happens, you will be forced to make those cuts anyway. If you wait to make the cuts, you will end up in an even worse predicament and might have even less wiggle room. Make the cuts now.

Making cuts in spending is more efficient than earning more money, which is an option we will discuss in the next chapter. The reason is taxes. If you cut $100 from your spending, your family will have an extra $100 to use elsewhere. But if you earn $100, you will have to pay taxes on those earnings, and you might be left with $70 or less to help your family.

MAKE A SPENDING PLAN

Most people do not like making a spending plan, also known as a budget. They feel it's too restrictive and they want to spend their money as they please. That will not work in a crisis. A crisis is one time a spending plan is an absolute necessity. At this moment, every dollar is precious and you must be sure you are getting the most you can with every one of them. The spending plan insures you will spend your money where you want it to be spent.

If you have a problem sticking to your plans, switch to using cash for purchases. Using a credit card is associated with 20% more spending than if you were to use cash. You feel you're spending more with cash.

In order to know what to cut and how much to cut, you need to know what you are actually spending. The form that follows is what I use to make a spending plan. You can download an Excel file copy from the "Recommended" tab on my website, FinancialSuccessMD.com.

SPENDING PLAN

A. Benefits Paid by Employer _____
  Retirement plan
  Health insurance
  HSA
  Other (_____)

B. Gross Monthly Income _____
  Salary
  Interest
  Dividends
  Other (_____)

LESS:

1. Tithe (10% of A+B) _____

2. Tax (fed., state, FICA) _____

NET SPENDABLE INCOME _____
(= Gross-Tithe-Tax)

3. Housing _____
  Mortgage (rent)
  Insurance
  Taxes
  Electricity
  Gas
  Water
  Sanitation
  Telephone
  Internet
  Maintenance
  Other (_____)

4. Food _____

5. Automobile(s) _____
  Payments
  Gas and oil
  Insurance
  License/taxes
  Maint./repair/replace

6. Insurance _____
  Life
  Medical
  Disability
  Other (_____)

7. Clothing _____

8. Debts _____
  Credit cards
  Student loans
  Other (_____)

9. Recreation _____
  Eating out
  Activities/trips
  Vacation
  Other (_____)

10. Medical Expenses _____
  Doctor
  Dentist
  Drugs
  Other (_____)

11. School/Childcare _____
  Tuition
  Materials
  Transportation
  Daycare
  Other (_____)

12. Miscellaneous _____
  Toiletry, cosmetics
  Beauty, hair stylist
  Laundry, cleaning
  Allowances, lunches
  Subscriptions
  Gifts (incl. Christmas)
  Cash
  Other (_____)

13. Savings _____

14. Investments _____

TOTAL EXPENSES _____

INCOME VERSUS EXPENSES
  Net Spendable Income ....
  Less Total Expenses − _____
  Discretionary Income ================

Start by listing your income and expenses for each month. Don't forget about the periodic expenses like quarterly insurance payments or property taxes. Next, calculate your deficit (income minus expenses). Cuts need to be made until at least income equals expenses. If you can't do that, the income shortfall will need to be made up using your emergency fund.

This works well if your crisis involves a significant drop in income, such as one spouse losing a job. If you have dropped to zero income, the cuts will have to be more drastic as you'll be relying on your savings until some income is coming back into the household. Since you are likely to get some government assistance if you have no income, it is unlikely your income will fall to zero, but it may for a short time.

Knowing the target to hit will help you as you start making cuts. Let's go through each of the categories on the spending plan and discuss possible actions to take. Remember, these are unusual times that call for unusual action. Also, remember this is not forever, just until the crisis is stabilized.

RETIREMENT PLAN

If you still have a job and are contributing to a retirement plan, tell the payroll department to stop your retirement plan contribution, even if you are getting a matching contribution from your employer. Your tax bill will go up since these contributions were tax deductible, but your overall available cash will increase.

Let's say you stop a $500 a month deposit into your 401(k). Your gross pay will go up by $500 and the tax man will take their share, say 30%, which leaves you with a $350 net increase in your monthly paycheck.

TITHING

I don't recommend you stop giving in a crisis, but it may be necessary. If your income dropped, then your tithe would drop commensurately. If you can't pay your bills, your tithe may need to drop to zero for a while.

TAXES

If you typically get a tax refund every year, increase the dependents you claim on your W4 to reduce the amount of taxes your employer takes out of each paycheck. You need the money now, not next April. Don't overdo this, however, and end up with a big tax bill you can't pay by paying too little taxes now. Your goal is to make the payments just right.

HOUSING

This category is one of the largest expenses in your spending plan, so it has the most room for cuts. You can talk to your mortgage lender about changing the terms of your mortgage or refinance the loan for a longer period or a lower interest rate. For some, forbearance is a possibility. You could stop paying your mortgage and hope for the best, since it will take a while for the bank to kick you out of your house, but I wouldn't recommend it.

If you're renting, you can talk to the landlord and see if they would give you a break for a short time. Don't stop paying your rent or mortgage without a conversation with the proper authority. Talk with the person you will not be paying and let them know what is happening. They may give you some leeway.

You can move to less expensive housing by selling the house you own and moving into a rental or buying a cheaper house. If your circumstances will be prolonged, this may be absolutely necessary.

You should be able to conserve on utilities. Lowering the temperature in the house in the winter and raising it in the summer will save money. Using less water and getting a smaller garbage container might help. There's no reason to pay for television service, as it's completely optional, even if you have kids. If you need internet service, you might be able to get it using your phone or visiting a neighbor, friend, or family member when needed. Many businesses and libraries offer free Wi-Fi. You do not need both a cell phone and a landline. You can also increase the deductible amount on your homeowners insurance to save some more.

FOOD

This is another stickler for some people. Many feel they must eat special food, food from a special store, or food grown in a special way. All of these special preferences make food more expensive. Save the special food for a time when you are not dealing with a crisis. I met one family who spent $500 a month on supplements, all of which could be cut out and no harm would come. If you miss your supplements for a little while, it will be OK. Shop for what is on sale. Look to the top and bottom of the shelves at the grocery store, as the most expensive choices are at eye level. Go for the basics and remember bulk beans and rice are a staple all over the world. Stop eating out. Take a sack lunch to work instead of eating out. Use the food in your panty. Do batch cooking and fill the freezer to save money by buying food items in bulk.

AUTOMOBILE

Most Americans spend far too much in this category. We love our cars and our car loans. Do you really need more than one car right now? Do you need a car at all? On the occasions when a car is needed, could you call an Uber? Increase the deductible on your car insurance. Sell a car and get rid of the payment or use the money to increase your savings. Walk, ride your bike, or take public transportation.

INSURANCE

In general, you can save money by raising deductibles and increasing the length of wait times before collecting on disability insurance. If you have cash value life insurance, switch to term insurance and pocket the cash value. Be sure you have the new term life insurance in place before canceling the cash value life insurance, or you could end up with no insurance at all. There is a reason you purchased that insurance.

CLOTHING

It is unlikely that adults will need to spend money on clothes during a crisis. Wear what you already have. Kids who outgrow their clothes will need to replace what doesn't fit anymore. Shop for kids' clothes at thrift shops, where you will find a lot of lightly worn clothes for great prices. Kids often outgrow their clothes before they wear out.

DEBTS

If you have been accelerating payments to get out of debt, you should stop immediately. During a financial crisis, only make the minimum payments. If the crisis gets really bad, since credit cards are unsecured, you can skip their payments with little consequence except to your credit rating and your pride. You may be able to do some renegotiating of interest and payments to save your credit rating. But that is secondary to surviving right now. Student loans can go into forbearance or change to an income-driven repayment plan. If you have debt payments on a toy, such as a snowmobile, motorcycle, motorhome, or boat, now would be a great time to sell the toy and get rid of the monthly expense.

ENTERTAINMENT/RECREATION

In a crisis, this section needs to go to zero. You should do fun things that are free. Playing games at home with your family, going to the park, or free days at the museum are good choices. You should not pay for entertainment.

If you don't have one, get a library card. Libraries have books to read as well as audiobooks. They also have videos and ebooks to loan. I listened to free audiobooks from Oodles Books when I walked for 38 days on the Camino de Santiago. There are also neighborhood little libraries where you can exchange books for free. Find one near you at LittleFreeLibrary.org.

MEDICAL

You might be tempted to skip the doctor or dentist. But if you or a family member has a serious problem, go anyway. Only minor things should be skipped, like teeth cleaning appointments or wellness checkups. If you are sick and need a doctor, get some help. Don't skip the kid's doctor appointments if they are due for vaccines. You do not want the kids to get sick because you skipped their vaccinations. Above all, don't let your health insurance lapse during the crisis. An injury in a car accident could really compound your problem if you don't have medical insurance.

SCHOOL

There is no place for private schooling in a financial crisis. It may also be necessary for your kids to skip other activities such as sports or music lessons, if they require a participation fee.

MISCELLANEOUS

There is very little you should need in the miscellaneous category. If it is not crucial, don't pay for it right now. You can go without a haircut or you can cut each other's hair. I'm sorry, but the housecleaner, the cook, the nanny, and the gardener have to go until you have recovered. Drop the gym membership and exercise at home. Stop buying bottled water. In most places, water from the tap provides free and safe drinking water. If you really hate the taste of your tap water, consider a filtered jug.

Keep a special eye out for hidden recurring costs that are automatically charged to your credit card or deducted from your checking account. These are things like Xbox, Netflix, HBO Now, cloud storage, antivirus programs, game charges from apps, on-demand cable programs, monthly music services, satellite radio, and other subscriptions. Often these are charged with a swipe of your finger or a quick glance using facial recognition. Many might also be free trials that start charging you soon without mentioning it again.

WHAT ABOUT MY BUSINESS?

Your business is a mirror of your personal financial life. You will need to go through a spending plan process with it as well. Cuts may also include employees. It is hard to cut people who depend on you, but it might be necessary. You can have employees use their paid vacation time now, take a partial cut in hourly pay, work fewer hours, or take some unpaid time off.

If you have to lay off anyone permanently, look to your least productive positions or people. Now is the time to thin the herd.

What about pivoting your business a little in hard times? During the pandemic, restaurants that could not serve in-house diners began takeout and delivery services. Physicians who could not see patients in person began doing telemedicine.

If you have business interruption insurance, now is the time to use it if you have slowed or stopped working.

Now is the time to make deep and ruthless cuts. If you make them quickly and stop the hemorrhaging early, during the golden week, you will have a lot more money available to weather the crisis. If you don't need it to survive, now is not the time to buy it.

Chapter 4

BE AGGRESSIVE AT CREATING INCOME

FIND A NEW JOB NOW!

When you are in the midst of a personal financial crisis, one of two things has happened: either you have a huge increase in expenses (cancer operation and treatment) or a huge decrease in income (job loss).

The social distancing to fight the 2020 pandemic created sudden job losses for millions of people all at once. But not every industry was shut down. Many were thriving. If you made personal protective equipment for healthcare workers, ventilators, hand sanitizer, or toilet paper, your factories were running overtime to keep up. You were hiring.

So even in a massive natural disaster, there are still job opportunities. My son worked for a retail company that was shut down. The next day he was working for a contractor helping build a house. One summer when I was in college, I got laid off from a job and the next day I was painting houses. If you want a job bad enough to do what it takes to get one, you are likely to find one. But you must take the bull by the horns and go get it. When many people become unemployed at the same time, the remaining jobs go to the workers who get there first. You need to get there first, during the golden week.

Most job loss situations are not so widespread. Don't sit idle even one day. Treat this with the same urgency you treated making the spending cuts. The sooner you have a new source of income, the sooner you get back on your feet.

Don't forget to file for unemployment ASAP. Having the little boost it provides goes a long way toward helping your family while you look for a job. You have been paying taxes and unemployment insurance for years; now is the time to collect.

When you cut expenses, as we discussed in the last chapter, you can't cut back to zero. There is a limit. The great thing about adding income with a job is the sky is the limit—you can add as much as you can find and do.

For physicians and other high-income producers, we must remember that getting back to work is our highest priority as it has the greatest economic impact on our household. If we are out of work for a couple of months, we might burn through our emergency fund. But if we are out of work for a year, we are likely to also lose our retirement fund.

Update your resume or curriculum vitae (CV) right away so you can put your best foot forward in your job search. Gather together all the paperwork you will need for a new job. For physicians, this is all of your credentialing documents.

WHAT NOT TO DO

Here is an example not to follow. My practice was about to hire a person at the front desk. There was a doctor in town who recently announced she was closing her practice. That doctor had one staff member I knew and liked. We met through our kids. I called her up to offer her the job in our office. She told me she did not want to take the job. She wanted to take three months off and live on unemployment. After her nice paid vacation, then she would look for a job.

There are two problems with her plan. First, unemployment funds are not for vacationing. They are paid by all the taxpayers to help those in dire need feed their families due to a job loss. Second, she missed a golden week opportunity. It takes time and effort to land a new job. She had a good one drop in her lap and passed it up. When her unemployment money ran out, our position had been filled and she had to start her job search from scratch.

MAKE A PLAN AND GO FOR IT

The summer after my high school graduation, I needed a job to make money for college. My family didn't have extra money to help me. Although I had a scholarship, I knew I would need to make some money. It wasn't that I wanted a job—I needed a job, and many businesses were in a hiring freeze due to the recession.

I put together a resume, made many copies, and hit the streets. Walking through town, I stopped at every business to ask if they were hiring. I filled out an application everywhere that would take one. This was when you still had to apply in person, long before online applications existed.

I hit pay dirt when I walked into the Red Lion Motel. The manager interviewed me and asked about my previous work experience and what job I wanted. I told him I would take any open job—dishwasher or manager, it didn't matter to me. He told me he wanted me to be a bellman. He explained the duties, and I took the job on the spot.

He then made a call and asked the person he called to come to his office. When he arrived, he was dressed in a motel uniform. The manager said, "Bob, you are fired. Turn in your uniform." The guy was stunned. Then he got mad, took the uniform off, and threw it at the manager as he stormed out, cussing. The manager handed me the uniform and said, "He was the old bellman. You are the new bellman. Put on this uniform and report to the front desk for your instructions." I couldn't believe what had happened, but I was happy to have a job.

Here's the point of the story: I treated getting a job as an emergency and I found one right away. Too many people play around with getting a job, as if they have all the time in the world. I only had three months to earn money before the summer was over. I could not delay a single day. Every day I didn't have a job was a day less pay to get me through the school year.

Every day you don't have a job is a day longer in crisis. Do you like the situation you are in so much that you would like to spend a few extra days in it? You need a job with a paycheck. Any job will do. You cannot afford to hold out for the right job, or the right kind of job, or a job in the right part of town. Those luxuries are for people who are not in the midst of a crisis. You can look for that job later, when you have recovered.

The sudden loss of a job can be devastating if you have no emergency funds to back you up. If you do have a big emergency fund, you can take a little more time to find the right job, but you better get on it today because those emergency fund dollars will run out soon and you better have a job when they do.

I have known people who were out of work for months and even years. When you ask them how the job search is going, they usually say there aren't any jobs out there. When you ask how many jobs they applied for last week, the answer is usually zero followed by an excuse as to why they were not looking last week. But they didn't put in any applications the week before either, or the week before that.

These people are not out of work because there are no jobs; they are out of work because they are choosing to be. They aren't doing what it takes to get a job. If they wanted work, they would be looking for work. If they aren't looking for work, one can only surmise that they do not want work right now—like my friend who preferred to take unemployment for a while.

Don't be too proud to take a job, any job, with a paycheck. If there are still businesses in town who don't know you are looking for work, then you still need to beat feet. Don't stop until you hit them all twice—not only the ones where you saw jobs posted online, but also the ones with no job postings. There are a lot of unadvertised jobs out there.

Don't limit your job search to only the town you live in. Today with online job applications, you can apply to a job anywhere in the world.

Search for multiple jobs at once. Don't apply for one job and wait for their answer before moving to the next. Apply everywhere and then take the job that hits pay dirt. Many jobs today are applied for online and the company never bothers to tell you if you didn't get the job. They simply don't reply. So don't sit around wasting your golden week waiting for an answer.

If your spouse is not working, they should be looking for a job also. With twice the lookers, one of you is likely to come up with a job before the other. You never know which of you that will be.

After you have made massive cuts in your spending, you can now get by with a much lower salary. You aren't limited to getting a job with the same pay as before. You have more options.

If you have suffered a big pay cut but not a job loss, you could look for a second job. There's no reason you need only work one job. If it isn't getting you what you need, then you need another one.

I teach people not to overwork. You need to leave room in your schedule for the family. But in a crisis, you might not be able to do that. You might need to work many more hours than you want, to recover from the disaster. Keep in mind, the crisis will come to an end and you will get back on your feet. Until then, you must work to recover from your crisis.

Doctors can work extra shifts, take a locums job, take other people's call, or moonlight at a different hospital in town or in a nearby town. Two big problems they face are licensing and credentialing. Even when they find a job, there will be a long delay to get a state license and hospital privileges. You can find a job the next day and still not be able to work for three months or more. It's all the more reason to start searching immediately.

The best way to combat the licensing issue is to first look for jobs in the states you already have a license. Send job request information to every hospital and physician's office of your specialty. These letters should all be in the mail during the golden week.

Doctors also can pivot their practice in a new direction by providing telemedicine, chart reviewing, doing paid clinical surveys, or helping with medical legal cases.

MAKE YOUR OWN WAY

In chapter 2, we discussed taking an inventory of your skills. If you don't find a job right away, it might be time to pull those assets off the shelf and put them to work. We live in a gig economy now and no one will bat an eye if you start doing some side work to get by while looking for a job in your field of training. It may feel odd for a surgeon to be an Uber driver or a house painter, but you need to do whatever is needed to feed your family.

Be sure people know about your gig. Advertise as a handyman, put signs up in the music store about teaching piano lessons, get registered as an Uber driver, or do whatever you need to do to use your skill set. Don't limit your options to only one skill. Advertise several skills at once.

No matter what you do, if you treat this like an emergency, you will get much better results than if you apply for unemployment and don't put much effort into finding a job. Get out there and find a way to provide for your family.

MY STORY PART 4: THE PLAN

During the third week of April, less than two weeks after losing my other job opportunity, I was scheduled to appear in person before the medical board in order to get my license to practice medicine in Oregon. I decided to use that trip to hunt for another job opportunity. Since there was nothing advertised where I wanted to live, I needed to look for what was not advertised. I would create my own opportunity. I would find a way.

After my Monday morning interview with the board, I began my job hunt in Portland and then drove south on Interstate 5, stopping at every town on the way to Medford, where I planned to spend Saturday visiting my parents before returning home. As I made my way south, I called ahead to each hospital and asked for the medical staff office, where I inquired about who the general surgeons were in town who may be interested in adding a new partner. I also called every surgical office in every town on the 270-mile trip and was able to stop in and meet several surgeons.

My Friday morning call to Grants Pass was interesting. There was a pair of general surgeons who needed a new partner, but they had already found one who was planning to join them in a few months. Coincidentally, the senior partner and his wife were leaving that day to spend the weekend in Sun River and decided that morning to drive instead of fly his airplane. Because they were driving, their schedule and mine would intersect at a nearby town, where they could take a short break to meet for coffee.

During their one-hour drive to the restaurant, the surgeon and his wife discussed all the aspects they were looking for in their new partner. The physician they had lined up to join them met most of those criteria. We had a longer visit than they intended, and I later learned I met every requirement on their list.

After I left the restaurant, I headed to Grants Pass, where I met the other partner and toured the hospital and their office. It turned out the junior partner trained at the same residency program I was about to graduate from, and we were both taught by the same chief of surgery.

I finished my journey by spending a day with my parents and then flew home without a good prospect for a job. But now I had hope. I had found job opportunities where we wanted to live that were not advertised.

What happened next blew my socks off.

Chapter 5

SELL SELDOM-USED ITEMS

In chapter 2, you listed your assets. Some of those assets, like jewelry, collections, art, and precious metals, could be sold to help generate cash to get you through the crisis. It's time to take a long hard look at which of those assets really bring you joy.

For example, I have a collection of limited-edition prints. Many are not hanging on my walls and are stored away as investments. I was hoping they would appreciate in value, so every time I found one I liked, I bought a second one for an additional investment. During a personal financial crisis would be a good time to convert those prints to cash that I could use to pay my bills.

I may not get top dollar if I need to sell them quickly. But selling a limited-edition print for $500 would mean my family could eat for another month. That is far superior to having the print hidden away, even if it is possibly continuing to grow in value, when I need its value now.

There are also less valuable things around the house that could be sold to generate cash. Cash is king right now. The bookcase full of DVDs, the treadmill that never gets used, a second car, and clothes that don't fit are all candidates.

It's likely you can look around your home, attic, closets, and garage and find things that could be sold in a garage sale or on eBay, Craigslist, Facebook Marketplace, or any other place people sell things in your city to produce quick cash.

Many miscellaneous items will not generate much cash, but some items are worth the effort, like a large collection of Depression glass or other collectibles.

I was recently decluttering our house and came across a collection of Yu-Gi-Oh! cards. When the kids were young, they were interested in Yu-Gi-Oh!, so I learned to play the game with them. I ended up with a large collection of cards. *(Participate in the things your kids are interested in and you will love the results. We played in several tournaments together and actually had national tournament rankings!)*

The kids had long ago outgrown the game, and the cards were gathering dust. I acquired cards by buying out card-trading businesses that were closing and I accumulated over 25,000 cards! I found a dealer who was interested, and I sold him my collection for $900.

It was less than I thought I should get, but the cards were worth nothing sitting in the closet taking up space. Had I been in the midst of a personal financial crisis, the $900 would have helped a lot.

Having a garage sale works for the little things, the cheap stuff. Since most people don't want to pay more than a few dollars for anything at a garage sale, that should not be the venue you use for the bigger ticket items or special collector's items. A garage sale is a good place for miscellaneous, low-value items like kids' clothing, books, and DVDs.

If you have an item with a limited customer base such as an autographed guitar, it needs to be advertised to the target audience. Things that are easily shipped can go on eBay. Things needing local pickup, like a couch, should go on a more local site like Craigslist.

If you have watched the TV show *Pawn Stars*, each show highlights people selling their treasures because they need cash. Often, they are special items needing special buyers. The item is presented to one of the employees of the pawn shop. They listen to the story about where the seller got the item, why they want to sell it, and what they think it is worth.

"My son is in college and I have this old guitar signed by Elvis that my father gave me 30 years ago. It was the guitar Elvis used in the movie *Blue Hawaii*. My father worked on the set with Elvis, and they became good friends. I thought if I sold it, I could pay the tuition for my son's next semester at college. It has been sitting in the back of the closet for years."

They haggle a little, make a deal, and the seller leaves with money in their pocket and a smile on their face. They converted an asset into cash they can use right now for anything they need.

Get ruthless and convert your unused or unneeded items to cash and use the cash to pay your bills. You also get the added benefit of decluttering your house.

Chapter 6

URGENT PROCRASTINATION

In chapters 3 and 4, I emphasized the need to treat spending cuts and finding new income sources as the emergencies they are. Take definitive action in the golden week, the first week after the crisis begins. Don't keep bleeding money while you figure out what to do.

Now I want to emphasize the opposite. There are things you need to urgently procrastinate. I know that doesn't make sense on the surface: urgent procrastination is an oxymoron.

WHAT TO POSTPONE

There are things you have scheduled that you should not do in the midst of your crisis. The CME (continuing medical education) trip to Las Vegas and the family vacation to Disney World are good examples. No matter how disappointed the kids might be, this is not the time to spend money on optional endeavors.

An elective surgery you have been planning, such as cosmetic dental work or an inguinal hernia repair, can wait a little longer. You are not likely to suffer if you put them off, but you will suffer if the money you spent turns out to be needed elsewhere.

This is not the time to think about replacing your car, unless it is to purchase a cheaper car to eliminate a payment or to capture the equity in an expensive car you sell. Never consider swapping to a car with better gas mileage as a money-saving strategy. The drop in gas expense between the two cars rarely has a good effect on your finances when offset by the expense of the new car.

Your crisis may require you to postpone your retirement date. Retirement is all about having enough passive income so you don't have to work every day. If your savings just took a big hit, you may not be able to retire as planned. You might need to work a few more years to rebuild your capital. An additional three years of work is three more years of retirement plan con-tributions, three more years for the stock market to rebound, three more years of accumulated interest, and three more years you were not taking money out of your retirement plans. All those threes can really add up!

This might be a reason to wait longer to take your social secu-rity. Every year you postpone, your social security income will be 8% higher when you do begin to take it. This only works until age 70, when your social security benefits stop increasing.

Minor home repairs will have to wait. No matter how bad the house needs repainting, it will have to wait another year. You might need to make an exception to this if your plan involves selling the house. If your road to recovery involves losing the house to the bank, don't make any repairs.

Some parents really go overboard planning birthdays and other parties. I have been to some very expensive parties for 3-year-olds. Those are not luxuries you can afford during a financial crisis. Scale back on the presents and the party. A homemade cake and a few friends over to play will have to do.

If your crisis happens near Christmas, you'll need to make adjustments to your gift-giving plans. Holiday travel might be out this year as well. Your parents will understand if you can't come for Christmas. If you fill them in on your financial crisis, they may even pitch in to help with your recovery.

If your crisis involves a crash of the stock market, that's another opportunity to do nothing. More money is lost by acting during a stock market drop, and locking in losses, than by procrastinating during a drop. Don't change investment plans based on what the stock market did today, last week, or is expected to do this week. Invest for the long haul and these blips won't matter.

The bottom line is to put off any expenses that are not absolutely necessary. You need to save cash for food and shelter, not vacations. You don't need to see the latest movie in the theaters. It will be available next year and will be just as new to you then.

WHEN DREAMS ARE LOST

(Dr. Christopher Yerington)

We always envisioned our life in a dual anesthesiologist household to be one of financial bliss. The original plan was for me to work my tail off and Lori to work a more normal 40-hour week, taking little call, so she could be home more to raise our two boys. This disparity of work meant my schedule brought in 70% of the household income. One of the agreements we made when we married was to run the household on 50% of our income. Little did we know how this decision would later become our saving grace when financial disaster struck.

My first financial wreck, the divorce from my previous wife, included a hefty child support agreement for my first two children. The financial ramifications of divorce affected my choice of cars, homes, and other material things. Consequently, I was in the best financial position of my life when my house of cards came crashing down at age 38.

The resurfacing of the effects of my traumatic birth injury resulted in the loss of the good use of my left hand. Thus began the second great financial calamity of my life:

disability. Unfortunately for us, the timing created the perfect storm.

My disability occurred in the aftermath of the 2008 market crash. When I realized I could no longer do the things required to be an anesthesiologist, I got scared and made some poor choices. We moved our portfolio to a more conservative position at exactly the wrong time, which meant locking in losses and missing the early stock market rebound.

We had real estate investments, along with deals in the making, when my income came to a halt. Some of the deals developed problems that eventually dropped my investment portfolio by seven figures.

We then discovered our financial advisor had been grossly overcharging us. Even though he got sanctioned and fined by the SEC, he did not return any of our money. We were very angry, but we moved on to a new financial team.

When my job ended, so did my health insurance. Because I now had a preexisting disease that could be traced back to childbirth, I became uninsurable. This resulted in my wife leaving private practice to take a faculty position at the university which came with a 33% pay cut but provided me and my family with medical insurance.

To top it all off, my child support agreement called for escalating payments. I always thought my income would increase over time. Now that arrangement became problematic.

I had both private disability insurance and group disability insurance, and combined, they replaced 47% of my previous income. Unfortunately, these policies did not kick in until I had been out of work for four months.

Fortunately, we had prepared for financial trouble by having an emergency fund of six months' worth of expenses. However, in our perfect storm we burned through that fund in three and a half months.

That first year we struggled with many adjustments, but one very painful moment was when I realized my dream of fully paying for my children's private college education was not going to happen. At the end of the first year of being disabled, my daughter was two and a half years from beginning her college education. The divorce had already hurt my college saving plans and now with our reduced income, we needed a new plan. My daughter started looking at more reasonably priced college programs. She understood our financial problem.

Our new financial advisor recalculated our retirement projections, which were very different from our previous projections. Turns out when you stop making retirement plan contributions, the retirement account growth slows considerably. We increased my wife's retirement savings to the company maximum but that reduced our useable monthly income stream.

With income on the lean side, we had to cancel our already planned vacations. Money I had set aside to purchase my dream car needed to be used for monthly bills, plans for some home repairs and remodeling took a back seat, and we raised the deductibles for all our insurance policies to conserve cash.

I remember chatting with some friends, one of whom happened to be a CFP (Certified Financial Planner), when I said out loud, "How did this happen?" The CFP replied, "Be happy it was your money and not your health." He didn't realize it was both—I had lost the good use of my left hand and lived in chronic pain. It was then I truly realized the financial dreams I had in medical school were gone forever.

We downsized our dreams and our lives in earnest. Almost a decade later, we still live in the same house because saving our home became our number one financial objective. We drive less expensive cars, and vacations have decreased to every other year. Lori works more hours now, taking call and doing hospital educational and administrative duties in order to maintain our income. I took over the lion's share of roles with the house and kids. We helped my kids from my previous marriage through college as much as we could. They are both in graduate school and now independent.

There was also a definite psychological component to all this change. I went from being a super go-getter working 100 hours a week to being a disabled physician working zero hours a week. I also lost the mentally stimulating interactions I loved having with my colleagues in the hospital. Yet we kept adapting and kept going.

In retrospect, our biggest problem early on was not treating this as a financial emergency with a full understanding that our circumstances and financial future had changed. We instead treated it solely as a medical emergency. The focus was on my hand and the worry of the problem worsening. The worry that I might possibly be in a wheelchair in five years overshadowed other concerns. We tried to keep our finances the same; the plans, the deals, the striving toward that imagined "financial bliss." Our resistance to accept our new normal lasted too long. We didn't want anything to change.

Tomorrow, my son turns 16 years old amid the COVID-19 pandemic. He can't get his driver's license because there is no in-car training available. Last night, we told him we are sorry that this is the way it is in the world right now, but tomorrow it will get better.

"I know, Dad, I absolutely know it'll be OK tomorrow because that's what you and Mom do every day. You guys make tomorrow better for the whole family." Yes, my eyes watered at that statement, secretly, back in my bedroom. My son made me proud of the manner in which Lori and I have bumbled through the biggest financial crisis of our lives.

By making consistent choices, we reduced our living expenses to about 75% of what they had been the day I lost my job. My disability income plus Lori's income now provide us a 25% per month cushion. It's not the same as the 100% cushion we started with, which I am so thankful we had at the time. I hate to think of how this would have turned out if we had not started from a position of financial strength. We now have new dreams and a new plan, but we have learned to be happy living our new normal. In the end, tomorrow did get better for us.

Chapter 7

USING YOUR EMERGENCY FUND

On our seventh day of walking the Camino de Santiago, we stopped in the little town of Ventosa, Spain. When I say little, I mean it had a population of less than 200. We checked into the six-room Hotel Rural Las Aguedas—what a wonderful oasis in this little village. The common room and dining room were filled with beautiful 150-year-old antique furnishings. At dinner, we learned the owner had retired and used her life savings to gut this incredible old building and turn it into a six-room hotel to serve the pilgrims walking the Camino. We loved the place so much we decided to take our first rest day there and booked a second night.

We departed from this beautiful spot before the sun came up because it was going to be a hot, sunny day. As we went down the staircase toward the entry, we heard rain. Covered with sunscreen and ready to face the heat, this was the last sound we expected. When we got to the bottom of the stairs, we discovered the rain was *inside* the building. Water was pouring out of the ceiling fixture and there were six inches of water on the floor.

We went up to the top floor to wake the owner. She sounded very unhappy we were knocking on her door so early. We told her there was a flood downstairs, and she jumped into action. I helped her find the problem, which turned out to be a third-floor toilet tank that had cracked and had been pouring water most of the night. I shut off the water valve going to the toilet, which stopped the water flow.

That room was completely flooded. The room below, on the second floor, had water coming down from the light fixture, which was a beautiful chandelier that had crashed down onto the bed. The foot of the bed was soaked, and water had flooded that room as well. The first-floor foyer and office were also flooded. Basically, everything on that end of the building was ruined.

She was in tears. It was about 6 a.m. on a Friday morning and another batch of pilgrims was expected to arrive that afternoon. She would need to contact all the pilgrims planning to stay with her and let them know she was closed. She needed to take pictures, contact her insurance agent, and find some contractors to repair the damage. The hotel with all her antiques was her only source of income, which would suddenly be stopped for an unspecified length of time. This disaster would also cost a lot to repair.

She had a lot to worry about that day. I hope she had an emergency fund for just such an occasion.

A January 2019 Bankrate survey (bankrate.com/banking/savings/financial-security-january-2019/) found some alarming but not unexpected results. Only 40% of Americans could pay for a $1,000 emergency out of their savings, yet 30% stated they or an immediate family member had a major unexpected expense in the past 12 months, and more than a third of those cost in excess of $5,000.

In their January 2020 survey (bankrate.com/surveys/financial-outlook-survey-january-2020/), they found that 43% of Americans thought their financial situation would get better in 2020. Only 16% thought their finances would worsen in 2020, and 12% planned to save more money for emergencies this year. Little did they know the world was about to come to a halt.

The majority of Americans are not saving for emergencies. Perhaps it's because we are always hopeful that things are going to get better, as the study showed.

If you are one of the those in the midst of a financial crisis and you have not stashed away an emergency fund, the horse is already out of the barn. During a financial crisis, you cannot save for the crisis—you need to have those savings in place before trouble hits. Many job losses and health issues come suddenly, without time to plan—thus the term emergency. If you have made appropriate plans, and you have a substantial emergency fund, now is the time to use it. Let's discuss how to get the most out of the money you have saved for this emergency.

THINGS ARE DIFFERENT NOW

The most important thing to remember about your emergency fund is this: don't treat it like just another paycheck. Use it sparingly. It is easy to access, and so it may get abused. Don't dip into it just because it's easy. It is for emergency use only.

The emergency fund is not your first line of defense. First, make the hard cuts and boost your income, and then if you are doing your best and have a little shortfall, use the emergency fund to make up the shortfall.

If you use the emergency fund first, that well will run dry. Once it runs out, you won't have any money to fall back on.

Consider it like a spare tire in the car.

I once hit a stick in the road and got a flat tire. I was out in the boonies at the time, heading for a hiking trail. I changed the tire and was now driving without a spare tire. There also was no cell service at this location.

It would have been foolish for me to continue my plans and drive to the hike without the comfort of a spare tire or cell phone service. I turned around and headed back into town to get my tire fixed. The hike could wait.

Another example is the backup electrical generator in the hospital. If the power fails, the generator comes on to keep ventilators and other crucial things running. Every department immediately cuts back their electricity usage to put less strain on the generator. No new operation can be started. We don't have a backup for the backup. If we were to start another operation and then the generator failed, how would we explain that to the family? "I'm sorry your mom died. We really wanted to get her operation done today so we started while on the backup generator. We thought we could rely on it."

Treat your emergency fund like a spare tire or the hospital emergency generator. If you use it, you must become extremely conservative. You cannot go on with business as usual and burn through your emergency fund at the rate you spent money before.

ACT LIKE YOU DON'T HAVE AN EMERGENCY FUND

Consider what you will do when your emergency fund runs out. What cuts would you make then? Act now and make those cuts before the money runs out.

It's a big mistake to say you would pull your kids out of private school if the emergency fund runs out and you don't have a job by then. If that is your plan, then you are not acting like you are currently in a crisis. Now is the time to pull your kids out of private school and conserve money so you do not reach a point where the emergency fund runs out. If you use your emergency fund to sustain your normal life, the funds might run out too quickly. You heard in Dr. Yerington's story in the last chapter how his six-month emergency fund only lasted half that time. Use the emergency fund to sustain a scaled-back lifestyle.

KEEP THE EMERGENCY FUND FOR TRUE EMERGENCIES

Another thing to consider is how you define an emergency. Too many people dip into their emergency fund for nonemergencies. They don't want to miss out on a great house that just came on the market, so they raid their emergency fund to come up with enough money for the down payment. That is a big mistake. When you do that, you no longer have the backup plan you need. Buying a house is not an emergency. Neither is buying a car or any other tangible item.

What will happen if you buy that house using your emergency fund and then the week after you move in, you have a car accident and can't work for six months?

Not being able to pay rent or not having the money for groceries because you lost your job is an emergency. Save these funds for a real emergency. Using them to keep your kids in private school is the same as taking the funds to buy a car.

Since you have done the right thing and stored your emergency funds in a cash vehicle, like a money market account, you have immediate access to the funds without taking a loss. The people who stored their emergency funds in the stock market were in for a shock during the pandemic shutdown when they couldn't work and the stock market was down. A double whammy.

Here's how you should tackle your money flow issue:

1. Make the hard spending cuts.
2. Earn more money.
3. Sell stuff you don't need.
4. Dip into your emergency fund.
5. Dip into your retirement plan. *(More on this in the next chapter.)*

Many people want to take the easy route and use their resources in the reverse order. They don't want to make the hard decisions on cutting costs, looking for employment, or selling unneeded goods, so they spend their emergency fund and retirement funds first. Then their reserves are gone, and they are forced to make the cuts anyway, and without any money in reserve.

Think of your emergency fund like a parachute and take very good care of it because you might need it in an emergency. Don't treat your parachute like the pilot in this story did.

THE PARACHUTE

Once there was a pilot who got in a bit of a money crunch and was looking for ways to cut expenses. He got a hole in his pants but didn't have the money to buy a new pair. He realized his pants were made of the same material his parachute was made from. A small piece of the parachute could be cut out and used to fix his pants for free and the chute would still function with only that little hole.

He made the repair. Then he fixed his wife and kids' pants. Over time, there were many things he repaired using the free material from the parachute, always thinking the little hole would not make a difference in the functionality of the parachute.

Then one day he had engine trouble in his airplane and needed to jump out before the plane crashed. He grabbed the parachute and jumped out of the plane. He pulled the rip cord and heard the chute open but did not feel his velocity change. When he looked up, his parachute looked like it was made of Swiss cheese. There were too many little holes to impede his fall.

Once you raid your emergency fund for a nonemergency the first time, it becomes easier to do again. Soon the emergency fund is all used up. The fund is empty and no longer able to help you in a true emergency.

When you do legitimately need your emergency fund, don't feel bad about using it. After all, this is exactly why you have an emergency fund. Be glad it is there to get you through and get busy resolving your crisis. After this crisis is over, refill the emergency fund before your next crisis hits.

Chapter 8

TAPPING INTO RETIREMENT FUNDS

I really hate to see anyone take money out of their retirement plans for anything other than supporting their retirement years. But in a true crisis, unusual times call for unusual action. Your family's financial survival right now takes priority over your future retirement plans.

In most instances, if you withdraw money from your retirement plan early, you will pay taxes and penalties for early withdrawal. That means this money is expensive to get and should be at the bottom of the list of ways to get quick cash. If you end up paying a 10% penalty and 30% tax, then for every $100 you take out of your retirement plan, you will only have $60 to spend. That is a steep price to pay. You also won't be able to put the money back into your retirement account to use in your retirement. Contrast that with the emergency fund. When you take $100 out of the emergency fund, you have $100 to spend.

Unfortunately, many people jump to the retirement plan alternative first because it is easy. They mistakenly treat it as if it were an emergency fund. It is not an emergency fund; it is your retirement fund. If you lose your job, you can go to the administrator of your retirement account and ask them to give you the money from your retirement account and they will write you a check. Just because it's easy doesn't mean it's the best thing to do.

When I was in charge of the retirement plan at a business I co-owned, I saw firsthand what our employees did when they needed money. Many of the people who got fired (crisis) would ask to have their 401(k) money so they could use it to live on while they looked for another job. I felt so bad cutting that check, knowing what they were really losing by taking this money. I often tried to talk them out of taking their 401(k) money, but no one listened. Everyone felt they needed their money to get them through until their next job started.

A less painful alternative is to take a loan from the account, if that is allowed in your circumstance. But you must still be employed by the company that has your 401(k) to do this. If you are not employed by them, you must have the loan repaid before they turn in their tax return data, or that loan will be counted as a distribution.

If you are still working, another alternative is to stop making retirement contributions until you are back on your feet. Your retirement account would grow more slowly, but you would have more money in your paycheck to use during your difficult time. This will avoid penalties and will keep your current retirement funds intact.

Exhaust your other alternatives before you raid your retirement accounts. As I noted in the last chapter, retirement funds are the last funds to tap. If you do take your retirement money, please seek the guidance of a good CPA before you make the move. You want to be sure you do everything right. You don't want to add trouble with the IRS to your current problems.

Following are the things you need to know about taking money out of your various retirement accounts. If the situation is right, you may be able to avoid penalties. I listed these in the general order of people's largest balances, not the best order to draw them down. Your best order to take these funds will depend on which ones you have, your current income level, your situation, and your age. Seek professional guidance for your individual situation.

401(K), TRADITIONAL IRA, AND OTHER QUALIFIED PLANS

If you take the money out before age 59½, you will pay a 10% penalty **unless you have one of the following situations:**

✓ Paying for qualified higher education expenses

✓ Purchasing your first home (you may take out $10,000 or less)

✓ Court imposed family support

✓ Early retirement (follow rule 72t, substantially equal periodic payments (SEPP))

✓ Death

✓ Disability

✓ Employment terminated at age 55 or older

You can also withdraw without the penalty for medical expenses under certain situations, but 401(k) and IRA accounts are treated differently:

✓ From a 401(k): for expenses > 7.5% of your adjusted gross income (AGI) in your current tax year

✓ From an IRA: for expenses > 10% of AGI in your current tax year

You may have the option to take a loan from your 401(k) account, if your employer allows it. This avoids paying taxes and penalties. The maximum amount that can be borrowed is half of your vested balance up to $50,000. This amount will need to be paid back to your 401(k) with interest.

Special considerations you may want to know about the CARES act of 2020 include these:

✓ There is no required minimum distribution for 2020. This will keep us from having to sell in a down stock market.

✓ If your plan allows for borrowing, you can borrow 100% of your vested amount up to $100,000 only between March 27, 2020, and September 23, 2020.

✓ The 10% penalty for early withdrawal from an IRA is waved for up to $100,000 for 2020 and the taxes owed can be spread out over three years.

ROTH 401(K) AND ROTH IRA

You can withdraw any contributions you made to these accounts, also known as the basis, at any time without penalty or tax.

If you are over 59½ years old, you can take all you want out of this account without taxes or penalties. This scenario is similar to the emergency fund. But use the emergency fund first.

If you are under 59½, you will owe taxes and penalties on the earnings unless A) You have had the account for at least five years and B) The withdrawal is used for these situations:

✓ Disability

✓ Death

✓ A first home purchase

You can take out the earnings without the 10% penalty, but still pay taxes for the following reasons:

✓ Higher education expense

✓ Up to $5,000 for a birth or adoption

✓ Medical expenses exceeding 7.5% AGI

✓ Early retirement (follow rule 72t, substantially equal periodic payments (SEPP))

✓ An IRS levy

HEALTH SAVINGS ACCOUNT (HSA)

This account can be used at any time for medical and dental expenses. If you have any unreimbursed medical or dental expenses, you can get them reimbursed with no consequences, even if the expense was incurred in past years. Just save your receipts to show the IRS if you are audited. Fill out IRS form 8889 for these withdrawals to avoid taxes and penalties.

If you are 64 years old or younger and you take the money out for non-medical reasons, you will owe income tax on the money plus a 20% penalty. This is even more expensive than taking money out of a qualified retirement plan.

If you are 65 years old or older, or disabled at any age, and take the money out for nonmedical use, you will only owe the income taxes on the amount withdrawn.

QUALIFIED TUITION PROGRAM (529 PLAN)

This account is set up for a particular person to cover their college expenses. In addition to college expenses, $10,000 can be used from this account for education below the college level. If the beneficiary is disabled, they can take the money out penalty-free but will owe income tax on the earnings distributed. Otherwise, there will be a 10% penalty imposed, plus taxes, on the earnings for any noneducational withdrawal.

One interesting way to get this money without paying taxes or penalties is to "sell" it to a relative. You can transfer the funds to a different student by changing the beneficiary to another member of your extended family. If you have a qualified family member who has the money to help you, but doesn't feel comfortable with a loan or gift, you can transfer the funds in trade. You could have them give you the value of the 529 account and transfer the account to them, so there's no direct benefit to either party. They gave you $10,000 in cash and you gave them a $10,000 transfer into their 529 account.

Let's look at an example. I need money now for a crisis. My brother has money but is worried that if he helps me financially, other family members will want help also. He doesn't want to show favoritism or open this can of worms. My brother already has a 529 plan for his daughter. I have a 529 plan set up for my son with $10,000 in it, but now I need that money. My brother and I can agree to exchange $10,000 cash for the $10,000 in my 529 plan. I change the beneficiary of the 529 plan to his daughter and he pays me the same amount for the exchange. The net effect of this transaction is that my brother has contributed $10,000 into his daughter's 529 account and

I have the $10,000 returned that I originally had in my son's 529 account. Each part of the transaction should be treated as a gift.

This is similar to your brother buying your second car for its current value to give to his daughter. He was getting her a car anyway and he just happened to get it from you.

Potential beneficiaries that your 529 account can be transferred to are your children, parents (or their ancestors), siblings, nieces and nephews, first cousins, or the spouses of those listed.

CASH VALUE LIFE INSURANCE

If you have cash value life insurance, you chose it so you could have a savings option in addition to permanent life insurance. Now you can either borrow against the cash value of the account and pay it back with interest, use the cash value to make the life insurance premium payments until the crisis is over and thus decrease your expenses, or close the policy and take the cash value.

Canceling the policy is not a good option if you still need life insurance. But you can purchase a replacement term life insurance policy for a lot less money and then cancel your cash value life insurance policy and take the cash value. You never want to be without life insurance if someone is dependent on your income.

CERTIFICATES OF DEPOSIT (FOR RETIREMENT OR NOT)

The money in a CD can be taken out early by paying whatever penalty is imposed. This penalty is small and is usually the forfeiture of the last few months' interest. This is the cheapest money to get ahold of by cashing out early.

Many people don't want to cash in a CD early for fear of paying a large penalty. But in the last few years, with interest rates so low, that penalty often amounts to very little. Often the penalty is forfeiting some of the interest you are getting. If your penalty for cashing in early is six months' interest, and you have a $20,000 CD paying 2% interest, then the penalty would be $200. That is a small price to pay to have $20,000 available to help you weather a crisis.

Since the bulk of the value of a CD is principal, not interest, there is little tax consequence to cashing out early. The tax ramifications are similar if you cashed out at maturity.

ANNUITIES

Cashing out your annuities before you are 59½ often means owing taxes on the earnings plus a 10% penalty. The insurance company that sold you the annuity might also have a surrender charge depending on how long you have had the annuity.

Check your contract for waivers. Some companies will allow you to take some or all of the money back in the event of disability, nursing home confinement, or terminal illness. Some companies let you access 10-15% of the value without penalty.

Chapter 9

TAPPING INTO YOUR HOME EQUITY

We paid off our mortgage in 2001, so for the last 19 years we have not had a mortgage on our house. Once you have tasted the financial freedom of not having a mortgage, you never want to go back into debt. Even though the equity in my home is a large asset, using it puts my place of living at risk. It is best not to think of your home as an investment or a piggy bank you can break into whenever you need money. You need a place to live and a paid-off house is a very secure option.

That being said, it is a reservoir of money we could tap to get us through a crisis. That is, of course, if the house was not lost in the event causing the crisis. There are several ways to get cash from the equity in your house.

To take advantage of any option involving a loan, you must still be in a position to be approved for the loan. A job loss could hamper your ability to get a loan. For that reason, if you can see a crisis coming, you might want to make the move before your financial situation changes. For example, if you know or suspect you will lose your job in three months, do your loan restructuring while you are still employed. If you are the manager of a business, you can often see the company headed down the tubes before the final collapse. Make your move while you still can.

If you are able to get a loan, you will likely be capped at borrowing 90% of the value of your home. Because loans are based on your home value, you will likely be required to have your home appraised before receiving a second home mortgage or line of credit. Be sure to spiff up the house and yard before the appraiser arrives.

If you have a home worth $500,000, you can usually borrow up to $450,000. If the balance owed on your first mortgage is $200,000, you can get an additional mortgage for up to $250,000.

Just remember if you borrow money, when the crisis is over, you will need to pay it back. Thus, loan options run the risk of extending your time to full recovery. Selling your home gets you the best bang for the buck, but it is the most painful to execute. Selling also takes significantly more time to accomplish and could be too slow to help you if the housing market is currently moving slowly.

If your crisis will be a long one, such as recovering from a stroke, then selling will work. If you are considering bankruptcy, look carefully at your state laws as this may be an asset that is exempt from loss due to bankruptcy. Don't forget the possibility that you will not return to normal, and if you have a prolonged decrease in income and can't make the payments on a new loan, you might lose the collateral. I would hate for you to lose your home.

HELOC (HOME EQUITY LINE OF CREDIT)

This is a line of credit against the value of your house. It is money the bank has agreed you can take when needed and will be collateralized by your house. It's not an actual loan until you take money from your HELOC. You are often able to borrow money a little at a time as you need it, with minimum monthly payments that grow as you incur more debt. This can be similar to having a credit card tied to your home. This will increase your monthly expenses.

SECOND MORTGAGE

A second mortgage will give you a lump sum loan and a fixed monthly payment for a set period of time. It is just like your first mortgage and will increase your monthly expenses.

REFINANCE FOR LOWER PAYMENT

If you have been making house payments for a long time, you have paid down some of the principal of the loan. The current monthly payments are based on the original amount borrowed. Refinancing the loan for another 30 years will likely lower your monthly payment. The new monthly payment is based on the new amount of principal and the new interest rate.

If your original 30-year loan was for $500,000 and now you only owe $300,000 and the interest rate is 4% for each loan, refinancing will drop your monthly principal and interest payments from $2,387 to $1,432 and save you $955 a month in expenses, but you will now pay that amount for the next 30 years, increasing the time it will take you to become debt-free.

Likewise, you could save money if you were getting a lower interest rate on the refinanced loan. If your loan is still at about the original $500,000 but interest rates have gone down from 4% to 3%, then refinancing will drop your monthly payment from $2,387 to $2,108 and save you $279 a month.

REFINANCE TO HARVEST EQUITY

Another way to use refinancing is to harvest the equity from your house. Taking the first example of a $500,000 original mortgage that has been paid down to $300,000, you could refinance the loan for the original $500,000 and your payments would be the same (assuming you had the same terms), but you would put $200,000 into your bank account to help you through the crisis. You would have recaptured the equity you have paid over the last few years at the cost of resetting your payoff date.

You can also borrow more than the original loan if your house has appreciated significantly.

REVERSE MORTGAGE

This option is available for people over age 62 who have at least 50% equity in their home. The lender will pay you a monthly payment and add each payment to the mortgage total for as long as you live in the house. When you die or move, the loan then must be paid back. Selling the house usually accomplishes that task.

If your home was paid off and worth $600,000 and you are 65 years old, you can (at the time of this writing) get either $1,243 a month paid to you for life or a lump sum of $143,054 with no monthly payments for the rest of your life. The older you are, the higher the payments, but not by much.

SELL YOUR HOME AND MOVE TO A LOWER COST-OF-LIVING AREA

There is a great discrepancy in home prices across the country. If you live in a high cost-of-living area, you can sell your house and move to a lower cost-of-living area. There, you can either buy a new, less expensive house or rent one, and pocket a lot of money on the sale as well as significantly decrease your monthly expenses.

According to Zillow, the median home price in California is about $550,000; Colorado is just under $400,000; but in West Virginia it is $108,000, and in Iowa it's about $152,000. The cost of living is sky-high in some cities, like San Francisco and New York.

SELL YOUR HOME AND RENT

You can put your home up for sale to give you a lump sum of money to get you through your crisis. By lowering the price of your house, you can make a quicker sale, but keeping the selling price at or above market value will return a bigger profit. But remember, if you are in a crisis you need as much money as you can get quickly. Do what you can to make the home look nice to get a better price and a faster sale. Selling a rundown house will return far less money.

Once it sells, you can keep the difference between the selling price and the fees and outstanding mortgage owed. Putting that equity in your pocket becomes your new emergency fund. You can now rent a place to live while you work on your financial recovery. Depending on what you rent, this will either lower or raise your monthly expenses in comparison to your prior house payment and upkeep, but the proceeds from the sale will increase your bank account balance.

SELL YOUR HOME AND DOWNSIZE

Another option after you sell your home is to buy another home costing significantly less and have a lower house payment, no house payment, and/or money in your pocket. When you get a smaller house, the expenses of owning the home also decrease, additionally helping your monthly budget.

For example, if you own a house worth $800,000 and still have a mortgage of $300,000, you have $500,000 of equity plus a mortgage payment. When you sell the house and pay off the mortgage and the selling expenses, you might have $450,000 cash. You could then buy a new house for $400,000 and have no mortgage and still put $50,000 in your emergency fund. A $50,000 cash influx combined with eliminating your monthly mortgage payment will substantially help you through your financial crisis.

SELL AND MOVE IN WITH FAMILY

We don't tend to relish the thought of having to live with our parents or even our adult children. Once we become independent it is hard to go back. But hard times can mean hard choices. This might be one of them. Selling your house, pocketing the equity, and moving back home to possibly pay nothing for rent can be a game changer during a financial crisis.

Take a look at your situation, your job prospects, where you live, your house size, your equity, and the effect of the mortgage on your ability to get by each month. If you need to use your home equity to get through the storm, you should be able to choose one from the above options that suits your situation the best. Difficult times will put you through some difficult choices. Sometimes it's best to bite the bullet and move your family to better pastures.

MY STORY: INTERMISSION

Now that I have told you all these great ways to improve your situation in a financial crisis, I should point out that I didn't think of any of this at the time of my lost job opportunity. I was 31 years old and had never lived through a financial crisis. I had heard stories from others but never had firsthand experience. I didn't have a clue as to the possible tragedy I was about to face as an unemployed physician looking for work. I wish I had read a book like this one to help me get through this uncertain time.

Just like Dr. Yerington's story in chapter 6, I was so busy thinking about having lost my future job that I forgot to think about what to do to financially prepare for an extended period of unemployment. In reality, I continued to live my life as if my financial situation wasn't about to change.

Had I been thinking ahead, I would have been preparing for the possibility of not having a job when my residency ended. Yes, Carolyn would still be working, but her income would only cover our current living expenses. It would not cover the cost of me traveling to job interviews. The airplane tickets, car rentals, food, and hotel costs would have to come from somewhere.

We had cash in our savings account since we were saving up for the down payment on a house when we moved, as well as a vacation at the end of residency. There was also a little money in each of our IRA accounts. (If you recall, in the early 90s, only $2,000 a year could be deposited into an IRA account.) I also had money in my retirement account at the hospital. The bulk of our savings was in our retirement accounts, making accessing the money very costly with steep penalties and taxes.

A plan should have been formed for our pending crisis. Just like when a hurricane is reported to be headed for my house and I have a week to get ready, we should have been getting ready for an extended period of unemployment. For the last three months of residency, we should have been conserving as much cash as possible, but we didn't.

Here are some of the things we should have done with the comfort of hindsight.

✓ Stop going out to eat

✓ Stop making payroll deductions to my retirement plan

✓ Increase the deductibles on our car and renters insurance

✓ Get the money back we contributed to our IRAs a few months earlier (you can take the money back before the tax year ends and it is as if you never made the deposit)

✓ Cut back on long distance phone calls (they charged for those back then)

✓ Cut back on the grocery bill and eat out of the pantry

✓ Stop making extra payments on my student loans

Those are the moves we should have taken to prepare for my upcoming unemployment. Instead, we charged full speed ahead, hoping we had enough money in the bank and that everything would work out.

Chapter 10

DEALING WITH DEBT

I am a big proponent of getting out of debt and staying that way, as life is so much easier without debt. It's so important I wrote an entire book about it called *The Doctors Guide to Eliminating Debt*. Since most Americans have debt, it will likely be a complicating factor in getting through your crisis.

If you are working to get out of debt, then you have been making additional payments toward your debt to pay it off early. During the crisis, you should cut back to paying the minimum monthly payment for all your debts. You must conserve your cash.

If you owe money to a creditor and realize you won't be able to make the next payment, understand that it is better to run toward a creditor than away from them. Fill them in on your situation before the payment is late. You will have more options when you warn your creditor than you will have after a missed payment.

I own rental real estate. For the first 12 years of ownership, I managed the apartments myself. There were times when tenants couldn't pay their rent on time and there were two ways they handled the situation. The first was to contact me before their rent was due to warn me and tell me their plan. The second method was to avoid the difficult conversation by avoiding me altogether.

The first response came from the responsible tenants. I was very willing to work something out with those people. By contacting me early, they avoided setting in motion some predetermined events that culminated in an eviction and took up a lot of my time. The second response required me to do the legwork to track down the tenant. I was not very interested in working out a payment plan with the irresponsible tenants. When it looks like you're trying to stiff me, my response will mirror that.

Treat your creditors the same way you would like to be treated if you were the creditor. Creditors have more leeway when they are warned before a payment is late. When you took on a debt obligation, you made a pledge to repay the loan. You gave your word. When something unexpected happens to make following through with your plan impossible, you need to go to the creditor, tell them your situation, and come up with a solution.

Some creditors will work with you and others won't. You can't control how they will react, but you can control your actions. Be responsible and you will get better results.

There are several ways to handle your inability to pay: work out an alternative payment plan, agree to lower payments for a while until you are back on your feet, lower the interest rate, go into forbearance (skipped or reduced payments while still having interest accrue), or default on the loan. Your creditor wants their money and is likely to work with you to achieve an agreeable method of repayment rather than risk not getting paid at all.

If your crisis is triggered by a natural disaster, the lender is well aware and is already working on the problem. They do not want everyone displaced from a hurricane to default on their loans. There also may be a special government assistance program put into place after a natural disaster. Your creditor will help you get this assistance.

Reread the contracts so you know what the consequences are for missed payments on each of your debts. Will you get a higher interest rate with a late payment? Is there a fine? How long before they will take your collateral?

Can you settle the debt for a smaller amount? A lot of lenders will look at your situation and realize they are not going to get all of their money back no matter what they do. So, they might settle for a smaller amount of money to avoid a total loss. Offer to pay off the debt for a lower amount than what is owed and see what they say. If they agree, be sure they give you something in writing stating you are paid in full and report the same to the credit bureaus.

If your loan has been turned into collections, you still have rights. Some debt collectors behave like bullies as they try to collect money at all costs. Keep in mind the restrictions they must follow: They can only contact you between 8 a.m. and 9 p.m., they cannot call you at work, wages cannot be garnished without a court order, and there must be no behavior that would be considered harassment.

There is a statute of limitations for debt collection. Every state has different laws and your debt will become uncollectible after the statute of limitations runs out in 2-15 years. Check the laws in your state. Beware of making any payments after the statute of limitations runs out as this will restart a new statute of limitations period for that debt. However, if you later come into money, it is a very noble action to go back and pay off creditors, even though you are no longer required to do so.

Your credit score is likely to suffer if you miss or fall behind on payments. Terms and prices for many financial products are dependent on how good your score is. A low credit score will hamper your ability to obtain credit and other privileges in many ways:

- ✓ Prevent approval on future loans except possibly those with the worst terms

- ✓ Hurt your ability to rent or buy a home

- ✓ Increase the security deposit on future utilities

- ✓ Limit or eliminate financing options on future cell phone contracts

- ✓ Increase future insurance premiums

- ✓ Possibly hold you back from getting a job

But you are in a crisis and frankly, your credit score takes a back seat to your survival.

Make decisions based on what will help you conserve cash to pay expenses until the crisis is over. Once your crisis has ended, you can begin the work of repairing your credit score. The score will be important during your crisis if you need to borrow, move, or get a new job, so don't totally disregard the effect of your decisions on your credit score.

Beware of interest-free loans, which can be dangerous. The lender is counting on you not being able to pay the loan off before the interest-free period expires. Then the interest may become very high. If you take one of these loans, be sure you can pay it off before the interest-free period expires. If you currently have an interest-free loan, know what the interest and payments will be when the interest-free period ends.

TWO TYPES OF LOANS

There are two distinct types of loans. Unsecured loans are given to you solely on your promise to pay them back. If you don't pay them back, the lender can go after you directly to get their money, by commissioning a collection agency to collect the debt or taking you to court, but the terms do not include specified collateral that they can take from you.

The second type of loan is a secured or collateralized loan, where you have pledged a piece of property like a house, a car, or a boat as collateral. If you don't pay, the lender will take the collateral and sell it to recoup their money. If that doesn't cover the full amount due, they may also be able to sue you to collect the difference.

If you are in a situation where you can pay some of the loans but not all, make the collateralized loans a priority so you don't lose the collateral. Order the collateral on each loan by its importance. Your home outweighs your boat, for example. Since the lender doesn't have much recourse on uncollateralized loans, they go to the bottom of the priority list, with credit cards at the very bottom. Start by making the payments on the debts at the top of the list and continue down the list until you run out of money for that month. Better to have a credit card canceled than a car repossessed.

BE CAREFUL WITH DEBT CONSOLIDATION

Debt consolidation sounds great on the surface, but it can be dangerous. If you consolidate unsecured credit into a secured loan, you put yourself at increased risk. An example is getting a HELOC to pay off your credit cards. You just put your house at risk to pay off a loan that had nothing at risk, simply to save a little interest. Also, if you consolidate your credit cards, now you have credit cards with zero balances and if you don't cancel the cards, you run the risk of getting even further into debt. Soon you will have the credit cards maxed out again, in addition to the consolidation loan, leaving you worse off than you were before you consolidated.

AVOID LOAN PREDATORS

Many businesses are built to prey on people in crisis. Examples include payday loans and car title lenders. These people know you are in a bind and will do almost anything and pay any interest amount to get some cash. They charge way too much for their "services" and you cannot afford to pay their high prices. You can't afford to lose your car when you can't make the payments to the predator, which is exactly what they are hoping will happen.

BEST WAYS TO DEAL WITH DEBTS YOU CAN'T PAY

Let's take a look at some of the options available for dealing with different types of debt.

SECURED/COLLATERALIZED LOANS
MORTGAGES

When you are not able to pay the mortgage, talk with the lender as soon as possible. You might be able to get a forbearance on the loan, which will let you avoid a few payments now that you will make up at the end of the loan period while interest continues to accrue. Often the person you speak with at a national bank has no power and must follow the company procedures. A local bank or credit union is much more likely to be flexible.

If the housing market has tanked, it is possible you owe more than the house is worth. This is called being under water. This will pose a problem with both selling and refinancing, which we discussed previously.

Foreclosure will eliminate your monthly mortgage expenses completely, but you won't have a place to live. This should be used as a last resort. In this scenario, you simply stop making mortgage payments, which will reduce your monthly expenses. The bank will take a while before starting foreclosure proceedings and it might take upward of a year before they take the house back. You would therefore live rent-free during that time, but you will lose the house. This is only reasonable if you don't have much equity in the house *and* the lender won't work with you to find a solution. If you have a lot of equity, you do not want to lose it in a foreclosure.

CAR LOANS

Very frequently, if a new car is purchased on credit, the car will be worth less than what you owe on the loan. In order to return the car and get your loan canceled, you will need to pay the difference between the value of the car and the loan amount. This can still be the best option to reduce your expenses. If you recently bought a $40,000 car, it might be better to pay the $3,000 you are under water and give the dealership the car back in order to stop the loan payments.

To figure out what your best options are, ask the lender what your current payoff amount is and check with Kelley Blue Book (kbb.com) to figure out what the car is worth. Then you can consider selling, trading in, or refinancing. They may also consider forbearance on the loan.

STORE LOANS

If you have either a rent-to-own agreement or financed appliances or furniture and you stop making payments, the store will want their collateral back. You cannot keep the stove if you don't pay for it. I suggest you talk with the store. They don't want the item back, but if you can't find a payment plan the two of you agree upon, you should take the item back to them and cancel the contract. Each contract is different, so read your contract and see what it says about nonpayment.

TOY LOANS

These loans are for items we really don't need but love to have like motorcycles, recreational vehicles, snow mobiles, boats, etc.

In a time of financial crisis, you certainly do not need toys, especially if they come with the added financial stress of a monthly payment. It's time to sell and get out from under the debt.

You can contact the lender to see about restructuring the deal, but I suspect you will not find a lot of help in the toy area. You will likely need to sell these items on your own.

CELL PHONES

Cell phones have become almost a necessity today and almost all cell phones are financed. Phone companies sell their phones to you with a small increase in your monthly bill. This increase is the price of the phone, which will be paid off in 24 months. Then you trade it in and start making payments on the latest phone. Those payments are buried in your bill every month so you might not notice. If you own a very expensive phone, you might be able to sell it and get a simple, cheap phone instead.

UNSECURED LOANS

CREDIT CARDS

Credit card companies are in the business of supplying unsecured credit. Thus, with more risk to them, they charge a higher interest rate. With such high interest, they have plenty of room to negotiate it down and still make a lot of money.

Contact the bank and ask to get your interest rate lowered. Since you could get a credit card from another bank that will likely have a lower introductory interest rate, they will almost always work with you to lower the interest rate.

They also have an extremely low minimum payment for outstanding debt. I once bought something large on a Visa and with a $12,142 balance, the minimum payment required was $121—which is only 1% of the outstanding balance. I'm sure if I made the minimum payments and they started charging me interest, the minimum payment would begin to climb. Your minimum payment might be manageable, so work to keep it current and protect your credit rating if you can.

In times of a natural disaster like the 2020 pandemic, many banks offer special assistance to victims of the disaster. They may defer payments, waive fees, or offer an extended payment plan. But you must contact them to get these benefits.

If you are unable to make payments, your card will be frozen and your credit score will take a hit. They will raise the interest rate and charge you late fees, but you are not likely to pay those either. So if a loan payment must be skipped, this is a better one to skip.

BANK LOANS

If you have an unsecured bank loan, do your best to work something out with them. Read the contract to find out what the ramifications are for late or reduced payments. What are the nonpayment penalties and what action will they take? How many payments must you miss before action is taken?

Contact the bank and tell them what has happened. They will offer to work something out. They want to collect their money. Late payments are better than no payments.

They can take you to court and get your wages garnished or put a lien on any property you own, like your house. Just because the loan was unsecured doesn't mean they can't turn it into a secured loan with the help of the courts.

Seek a solution before they take action. If they take you to court, it will cost you a lot of time, money, and hassle.

FAMILY OR FRIEND LOANS

This is a touchy subject, but it's also the loan with the most flexibility. Your family will usually go to great measures to help you get through a crisis, especially if it is not a recurring theme in your life.

Do not avoid having this hard conversation. I have loaned money to family and friends and when they have a problem paying it back, they fall into the same two camps we discussed earlier concerning rent—either they reach out proactively or they avoid me. With the one who avoids me, when payments stop so does their presence at gatherings. Those people usually drop out of my life forever. It's hard to go to Thanksgiving and sit down for dinner across from the person you stiffed.

It is usually humbling to admit your crisis, but if you do, a solution will present itself. You can then agree on a new plan and Thanksgiving dinner won't be destroyed. Ask for a pause in payments or a temporary interest rate drop. Often a family or friend lender will be very generous to you, sometimes to the point of forgiving the loan, but only if you talk to them.

IRS

You never want to owe money to the IRS. They are a mean and ruthless lender. But can you blame them? Usually if you owe them money, the deal was not mutually agreed upon. The reality is you unilaterally told them you were not going to pay your bill, and thus borrowed money from them without their permission.

Imagine what would happen if you snuck into your mom's purse, took her credit card, and charged $10,000 on it because you wanted something. She didn't agree to the loan and she will be very upset, especially when you tell her you don't plan to pay it back until you get back on your feet.

If you can't afford to pay your taxes, still file your tax return or an extension anyway and avoid a failure to file penalty. That is an expensive tax you never need to pay. The penalty for failure to file is 5% of the unpaid balance, per month, up to 25% of the unpaid taxes. They will also tack on significant penalties and interest for failure to pay the tax due on time. That will be an additional 0.5% per month up to 25% until the tax is paid in full.

Again, just like other examples of this recurring theme, you need to contact them before you get on their bad side, not after. This has happened to many taxpayers, so the IRS already has programs in place to help.

You may qualify to apply for a long-term payment plan online if you owe $50,000 or less in combined taxes, penalties, and interest, and have filed all required returns. If you owe less than $100,000 in combined tax penalties and interest, you can file for a short-term payment plan online.

Go to the following website: https://www.irs.gov/payments/online-payment-agreement-application to apply online. Those ineligible for an online payment plan may still be able to pay in installments by filling out form 9465, the Installment Agreement Request. You also have the option of applying for hardship relief to get a compromised or canceled payment.

The IRS will also work out deals to settle the debt for less than is owed, or at least take off the penalties and interest.

Once you are in debt to the IRS, it is hard to resolve and there are many layers of red tape before you are labeled "paid in full." If the IRS labels you a "seriously delinquent" taxpayer, you could have your passport restricted and be unable to travel abroad.

It is best to avoid IRS debt entirely by transferring the debt to a different loan source. You can borrow from a friend or relative, get a personal loan, borrow from your retirement plan, use money from your IRA without penalty (but you still owe income tax on the withdrawal if indicated), or use a credit card to pay. Find a way to avoid falling behind in your tax obligation. Then make changes as needed so you will not owe money next year.

MEDICAL DEBT

Medical debt is the number one reason people file for bankruptcy. Financial hardship due to medical bills is very common—over 40% of Americans reported they suffered from it in 2019 (Yabroff, K.R., Zhao, J., Han, X. et al. Prevalence and Correlates of Medical Financial Hardship in the USA. *J. Gen. Intern. Med.* 34, 1494–1502 (2019): https://link.springer.com/article/10.1007/s11606-019-05002-w).

Medical debt is a little different from other debt. With a standard loan, you borrow a fixed amount under specific terms of repayment. Both parties agree upon the deal. When you go to the hospital, you have no idea how much your medical expenses will be, yet you agreed to pay. You didn't know the amount or terms of what you were agreeing to when you entered into the agreement. It's like signing a blank check. Consequently, there is room for negotiation.

Scrutinize your bills and make sure they are correct. Hospital bills have so many charges, there are always errors to be found. Find out if the hospital provides charity services and see if you might qualify for forgiveness or a bill reduction. You can ask for a payment plan and often it will not have any interest charges. Most hospitals also have an income-driven hardship plan available.

Years ago, my grandmother was the head of an Eastern Star (a subgroup of the Masonic Lodge) committee that helped pay people's medical bills. She asked me to help her find needy people who were deserving of help with their medical bills (no self-inflicted medical problems). She would then make arrangements to go to the hospital and make a payment on their bill. Her group had a cap of $25,000 per gift.

No matter the size of the medical bill, my grandmother would go to the billing department at the hospital and negotiate the price down. For example, if the medical bill was $45,000, she could get it dropped to $25,000. At first, the hospital representative wouldn't budge. Then Grandmother would point out the patient has no insurance and no money. If they insist on charging the $45,000, they will likely get nothing. If they would be willing to drop the bill to $25,000, their charitable organization would be happy to pay the bill. The hospital agreed to this every time.

The same concept applies to your physician's office. They will likely work with you if you have a problem paying them.

Since medical debt is more flexible, don't consolidate this with other debt or borrow from elsewhere to pay this debt. Let it stand alone.

STUDENT LOANS

Student loans also have different rules than other debt. If you are still paying on student debt when your crisis strikes, you must consider these special options.

Student loans come in two forms with different rules: private student loans and federal student loans.

Private student loans are essentially treated like every other type of loan you have and will usually declare you in default after three months of missed payments.

Federal loans have several forgiveness programs available that usually entail working for specific employers for a specified time while making reduced payments and then having the balance of the loans forgiven. Medical students often amass huge loans during training and residency, and often don't make enough money to pay the minimum payments for the loans. So, federal loans have a plan for the low-income years, allowing the students to make smaller payments during their residency based on their income. When they get their attending job, the payments will increase accordingly. The federal loans also have deferment and forbearance programs.

Do not stop making payments. If you go into default, you lose eligibility for most of the options available to you. For most federal loans, default will occur after nine months with no payments.

You have the option with your federal loans to go into an income-driven repayment plan. These plans will cap your payments based on your current discretionary income. If your income is low enough, the payment could even be zero. If filling out some paperwork could take your payments to zero, there is no reason to default on the loan.

Bankruptcy is not an option for this debt, as it is seldom discharged this way.

Debt is a thorn in your side when you have a financial crisis. Becoming familiar with the programs available to help you for each different type of loan can decrease the pain. During a crisis, you will really begin to understand what Solomon teaches in Proverbs 22:7 (NIV):

The rich rule over the poor, and the borrower is slave to the lender.

Chapter 11

GOVERNMENT AND OTHER ASSISTANCE

Most people who have been doing well financially have never needed government assistance. Then one day, disaster strikes and for the first time in their lives, they are in need of help. If a company as large as Chrysler needed help from the government, then you and I could certainly run into trouble that would leave us looking for their help.

Don't feel ashamed to ask for help. Government programs are designed as a safety net when trouble strikes. Whether you are in a natural disaster and FEMA is coming to the rescue, or you lost your job and need help with food and rent, there are many government programs available to help.

Your pride could stand in the way of getting the help you need, like it did for me during my first year of medical school. This was a time when I lived on less than nothing, as in using student loans to eat and put a roof over my head. One of my fellow students pointed out that we qualified for food stamps—the equivalent of SNAP today (see below).

I remember telling him I was eating just fine and didn't need food stamps. I thought it would be better to let other less fortunate people use the food stamps. Who is less fortunate than someone who is borrowing money to eat? I wonder if I would have felt differently if I was using my credit card to buy groceries and having to make payments every month. Did not having to make any payments on the money I was borrowing cloud my judgment? Did I have Debtabetic Neuropathy? (You can read about that in *The Doctors Guide to Eliminating Debt.*)

As I look back, I should have taken the food stamps. I think I got hung up thinking government assistance was only used by "poor" people and I was not a "poor" person. But I don't think I could have gotten any poorer than having to pay all my expenses with credit. I was in fact getting government assistance in the form of student loans. Somehow, I didn't see the government assistance I was getting as being the same as other government assistance. In fact, they were exactly the same. Both were a government handout for those in need.

Each government assistance program has different requirements for eligibility. You might qualify for one but not another. Check into all of them that might apply to your situation.

If a disability was the cause of your crisis, a lot of governmental programs will open up to you. If it was a natural disaster, almost everyone qualifies for some type of help.

When the 2020 pandemic caused a global shutdown, Congress quickly set up new programs to keep the economy going: Coronavirus Aid, Relief, and Economic Security Act (CARES) was one of them. Sometimes things change so fast it's hard to keep up. If you want to explore what you might qualify for, go to benefits.gov for more details. You would be surprised at what is available, such as the Emergency Assistance Livestock, Honey Bees, and Farm-raised Fish Program (ELAP). Who knew?

Don't forget about veterans' programs. If you are a veteran and have never used any benefits, now is a good time to find out what you can get. This is especially true if you have become disabled. Contact VA.gov to look into your eligibility.

Here are some of the main governmental programs available. Also look into local help for your specific problem. There are hundreds of assistance programs available.

GOVERNMENT ASSISTANCE PROGRAMS
CHILD NUTRITION PROGRAM

Provides free or reduced-cost lunches to school children. https://www.ers.usda.gov/topics/food-nutrition-assistance/ child-nutrition-programs

CHILDREN'S HEALTH INSURANCE PROGRAM (CHIP)

This is for children only and covers hospital care, medical supplies, tests, and preventative care. https://www.healthcare.gov/medicaid-chip/childrens-health-insurance-program

EARNED INCOME TAX CREDIT (EITC)

Tax credit for low-income families. Don't forget this one if you have a big drop in income. https://www.irs.gov/credits-deductions/individuals/earned-income-tax-credit

LOW INCOME HOME ENERGY ASSISTANCE PROGRAM (LIHEAP)

Help with energy bills. https://www.acf.hhs.gov/ocs/programs/liheap

MEDICAID

Medical care for low-income and disabled people. This program may even pay bills that predate your application. https://www.medicaid.gov

SMALL BUSINESS ADMINISTRATION LOANS AND GRANTS

Bridge loans and grants for businesses in need. Special new programs were introduced during the COVID-19 pandemic. https://www.sba.gov/funding-programs

SUBSIDIZED HOUSING PROGRAMS (HUD, UCAN)

Provides housing payment assistance. https://www.hud.gov/topics/rental_assistance, http://www.ucancap.org/index.php/what-we-do

SPECIAL SUPPLEMENTAL FOOD PROGRAM FOR WOMEN, INFANTS, AND CHILDREN (WIC)

Food program for pregnant women and children up to age 6. https://www.fns.usda.gov/wic

SUPPLEMENTAL NUTRITION ASSISTANCE PROGRAM (SNAP)

This is a food assistance program. https://www.fns.usda.gov/snap/supplemental-nutrition-assistance-program

SUPPLEMENTAL SECURITY INCOME (SSI)

Provides income for the disabled who have a condition expected to last longer than a year or which might result in death. Payments begin from the time of application, so if you think you might apply, do it early. https://www.ssa.gov/ssi

TEMPORARY ASSISTANCE FOR NEEDY FAMILIES (TANF)

Provides financial assistance in times of need. https://www.acf.hhs.gov/ofa/programs/tanf

PRIVATE PROGRAMS

There are also privately run programs, usually through non-profit organizations.

CHURCH BENEVOLENCE FUNDS

Your church may have a program to help those who hit a bump in the road. Ask.

GOSPEL RESCUE MISSION

A place to go if you have lost your home. Look for one in your local area.

LOCAL FOOD BANKS

If you are registered with a government assistance program, you can get food at the food bank.

Chapter 12

FRIENDS AND FAMILY

Friends and family can be valuable resources during a crisis. But because of the long-term relationships they provide, you must be careful how you proceed. You run the risk of creating a riff in the family if you handle this poorly.

UNDERSTAND WHAT'S AT STAKE

There's always a risk of losing friendships when money is involved.

A good friend of mine ended up in a severe financial bind. After he lost his job and had most of his possessions stolen, his crisis took him to ground zero. He needed money to move back home, get a suit for job interviews (the one he had was stolen), and restart his life. I decided to help him out.

I wasn't in a great financial place myself as a medical student, but I was better off than he was at the time. I agreed to loan him money to buy a new suit and a bus ticket to his grand-mother's home, where he would live and start his life over. We agreed on terms for this small loan.

After he got a job, he sent me a check for the first payment on the loan. The check bounced. He never contacted me again. What had been a great friendship since high school was sud-denly gone. He stiffed me on the loan and dropped our friend-ship. A few years later, he was in his own home with his new wife and child. He had the money to buy a car and a boat, but not the money to pay back the loan from me. He later moved within 30 miles of where I live, but he doesn't plan to ever contact me again. All over a few hundred dollars.

So if you decide to take a loan, don't do what my friend did. Pay the loan back as soon as you can. Relationships are far more important than a little bit of money. So be careful. Also, be sure both parties fully understand the terms of the loan.

Your friends and family can provide a lot of assistance. Moving back home with parents is certainly not desirable but might be necessary. Sometimes it is the best way to get through a crisis. My grandmother had a stroke in 2006 and moved in with her daughter for a year as she recovered. It was a huge help for Grandma and saved her a year's worth of nursing home bills.

If you move in with your parents, not only can you save a for-tune in housing costs, you might also save on childcare. Most grandparents would love to have daily time with their grand-kids. The national average cost of full-time daycare at a center is $972 a month per child. If you could save $2,000 a month in housing costs and nearly $2,000 a month in childcare costs for two kids, that comes to $48,000 a year. If you are work-ing to earn that money, you might need to bring in $70,000 to net the monthly savings you got from moving back home. That can speed up your recovery immensely and doesn't even include savings on utilities and food.

If you do move in with friends or relatives, set some ground rules. What parts of the house will be private for each party? How will you utilize the refrigerator? How are you paying for groceries? Will there be rent owed? Is there a curfew? If ev-eryone understands the rules, there will be a better chance of striking harmony.

Often friends and relatives are reluctant to give you money, especially if having a crisis is a recurrent theme for you. In that case, they may be able to provide you some time or other re-sources instead of money. A few examples are childcare, the use of their car, children's hand-me-down clothes, the use of their RV, groceries, or gas for your car.

Friends and relatives are great people for seeking advice. Financial disasters are not rare, so your friends and relatives may have already lived through one themselves. Seeking their advice also gives you a chance to air out your frustrations. Talking things over with someone other than a spouse, if you are married, can give you a different perspective. They will also feel flattered that you trust their opinion enough to seek their advice.

Once your friends and family know of your problems, they can become a big support system by giving both good suggestions and monetary help.

You will never know what they can do for you until you ask.

Chapter 13

WHAT NOT TO DO

When considering all the things you must do to get through a financial crisis, remember there are a few things you should not do as well.

DON'T PANIC

Panicking doesn't help in any situation. Earlier I talked about Batman and Robin. Here's the standard pattern for that duo: Robin tends to panic when things go wrong, but Batman stays calm and thinks about how to solve his problems. You need to be more like Batman. My son is a big Batman fan and has a shirt that says this:

Always be yourself! Unless you can be Batman - then always be Batman!

That may be a bit extreme, but you get the idea.

When we saw the toilet paper shelves empty during the start of the 2020 pandemic, it was a sign of people in panic mode. Hoarding things like toilet paper will not get us through a crisis. It also hurts those around us. Some people actually ran out of toilet paper that week and went to the store to find empty shelves. Your actions can hurt other people when you panic.

When the stock market drops, rushing to sell is a show of panic. Selling causes the market to drop even further. Since you know the stock market will drop periodically, you should plan for it to happen. If you panic when it happens, then you were not investing appropriately. Being ready for what could happen is a good way to avoid panic.

What if you made a mistake and were not ready for the crisis? There is still no need to panic. Calmly think about your options and pick one.

Just do the next right thing.

Buying gold to hoard is another panic move. If you think gold is a good investment, you should have purchased it long before the panic set in, not now that a crisis has happened. Whenever the stock market tanks, the number of commercials for buying gold skyrockets. Why would the companies that have the gold pay a celebrity for a national advertising campaign to sell their gold? They are the experts and they're not buying; they're selling. They are trying to convince you to buy the gold they own. They are taking advantage of your panic. Don't fall for it.

DON'T COMPLAIN OR BLAME

It is so common to hear more complaints during times of crisis. Now is not the time for complaining about how the system works, or what the political party in power is doing or not doing, or even what caused the situation you are in.

Now is a time for action. You are in the midst of a crisis you need to resolve. Spend your time and energy solving your problems, not complaining about them. You will be much better off emotionally if you concentrate on the good things you do have, rather than complain about the things you don't have.

When the crisis is over and you have recovered, then you can look back to see how you can make changes that might prevent or lessen the effect of the next crisis.

As I write this, we are currently in the middle of a pandemic. Many of the news reporters and politicians are busy complaining about what others should have done differently. They are working hard to pin the blame on someone. The blame game has no place in a crisis. They should be discussing what we're going to do to stop the pandemic and recover. Sometime after it is all over would be a good time to look back and see what we could have done better—not to pin the blame, but to find ways we can be better prepared next time. Include yourself and your spouse on the list of people not to blame.

DON'T IGNORE OBLIGATIONS

If there are things you agreed to do before the crisis, see to them during the crisis as well. You may need to cancel those obligations, but that is not the same as ignoring them.

This also applies to financial obligations like bills, rent, and debt. I covered this extensively in the debt chapter.

This is not the time to hide your head in the sand and ignore your obligations. Life doesn't stop because you are having a meltdown. Life goes on and when this is over, you'll still be going on as well. If you ignore obligations you made before the crisis, you will burn bridges you might need once the crisis has ended. Be careful to not burn any bridges.

Remember there is a big difference between "can't" and "won't." If a tenant doesn't pay rent and didn't contact me, I feel very different about the person who had a stroke and is lying in the hospital unable to speak, compared to the person who lost their job and didn't bother to tell me they couldn't pay rent.

The first person *can't* deal with their rent because of their hospitalization and the other *won't* deal with their rent. My response will be different for each of them even though the problem, nonpayment of rent, is the same.

DON'T GIVE UP YOUR HEALTH INSURANCE

Medical problems are very expensive and can get people into serious financial difficulty. Don't lose continuity of health care coverage if there's any way to avoid it. If you lost your job and you let the coverage lapse, when you apply for a new plan, you may have the problem of preexisting diseases to deal with.

Do what you can to keep yourself covered, even if it requires going to a high deductible health insurance policy. Job loss may open up access to your state health insurance options created by the Affordable Care Act.

DON'T STOP PAYING UTILITIES

Having your power, water, or garbage services canceled in the middle of your crisis really heaps on the trouble. It's hard to get a job if your computer is dead and you can't take a shower. Make paying utility bills a priority.

There are government programs to help pay for utilities if your situation is dire. Seek them out and keep the lights on.

DON'T STOP HAVING FUN

No matter how bad the situation, you still need to take time each day to have fun and laugh. Laughter is great medicine for your soul. Spending all your time worrying about your problems does nothing to help you or solve the problems. But spending a little time away from your problems having fun with your family will help you all.

Fun doesn't have to cost money. You can walk in the park, take the kids to the playground, play hide and seek, go to the free concert in the park, attend church services, have friends over to play cards, or go for a family hike. These are all activities that cost nothing, relieve stress, make memories, and give everyone peace of mind.

DON'T ALIENATE YOUR FRIENDS

We all need to feel connected. Hanging out with friends doesn't need to cost money, but it still needs to happen.

If you hit a financial bump in the road, you may feel embarrassed to tell your friends. If your friends always get together for lunch at a restaurant, tell them you still want to get together but can't afford the restaurant right now. If they are true friends, they will understand and find a way to get together that is free. Meet at the park with your sack lunches, play a round of Frisbee golf, or maybe even take a hike together.

Find a way to stay connected to your social network—your real social network, not the one on Twitter or Instagram. We all need support from our close friends.

DON'T DROP HEALTHY HABITS

Now is not the time to give up your exercise routine. You need to stay fit, and the endorphins you generate while exercising will make you feel more energetic and able to tackle your problems.

Continue to eat healthy. Just because your budget is limited doesn't mean you should buy poor quality food. Good food is not expensive. Specialty food disguised as good food is expensive. To save money on the food budget, you might need to stop buying things like organically produced or name-brand food. If you only have a limited amount to spend on food, buy nutritious food and not convenient junk food.

It is also very important to get enough sleep. I know when my life gets busy, I tend to sacrifice sleep. But when I do, I'm too tired to function efficiently during the daytime. Sleep is a very important part of staying healthy.

DON'T STOP PAYING TAXES

I mentioned earlier the trouble you get into when you owe money to the IRS. If your income drops significantly, so will your tax bill. It might even go to zero like mine did the first year I retired from medicine. Just be sure you have a good handle on what your taxes should be and don't fall behind.

DON'T DO STUPID STUFF

Often when things get tough, we start grasping at straws and doing things we normally would not have done. Now is not the time to start buying lottery tickets, laying on the couch all day in front of the TV, or robbing a bank.

Do not suspend your moral compass in desperate times like Walter White did in the TV series *Breaking Bad*. Right and wrong have not changed and neither have you. Your situation might have changed, but you haven't. Don't become something you are not simply because you are going through hard times. Unless you can be Batman!

If you do find yourself with a lot of free time, do something useful with that time. Learn a new job skill, volunteer somewhere, learn to play a musical instrument, learn a new song if you already play, or spend more one-on-one time with your kids. Take advantage of this opportunity to better areas in your life that require time you normally don't have. Come out of this crisis a better person.

DON'T STOP GIVING

Giving is good for you. The act of giving makes you a happier person. When you give, you feel like you have more. The giver often feels better than the receiver. When I am giving, I feel blessed and truly understand what Jesus said in Acts 20:35 (NIV):

"It is more blessed to give than to receive."

Those who have are the ones who give, and if you give, then you must be one of those who have.

A friend of mine was making a Christmas gift box for a needy family. He had been talking about how bad his financial situation was when he realized he was on the giving side of the Christmas boxes, not the receiving side. He realized that even though he had much less than he desired, he had a lot more than most people. He suddenly was aware of how blessed he was.

If you tithe, don't stop. Your income determines your tithe, so if your income drops, so would your tithe. Tithing is giving the first tenth of your earnings. If your income falls to zero, your tithe falls to zero. If your income fell to one half of what it was, your tithe will fall to half of what it was.

You can also give of your time. In fact, if you lost your job, you might be able to give a lot of extra time for a while.

DON'T GIVE UP

Lots of people have been in your shoes. Tough times happen more than you realize and this time it is your turn to endure. Don't despair. This too shall pass. What you are going through right now is merely a small part of the story of your life. It is not your defining moment.

Many people who face severe financial difficulty go into depression. They give up and are still unemployed and on government assistance a year later. Some even take their own lives. There is no need for that. If you are feeling overstretched and suicidal, reach out to hotlines, National Alliance for Mental Illness (NAMI), or state or local resources. Mental health care can be free or very low cost and it may save your life. If you know someone struggling with a financial crisis, give them this book, before it's too late.

If your actions were the cause of your predicament—by doing something you shouldn't have done—you can be the solution as well. Don't wallow in the blame. Shake it off and figure out what is the next right thing for you to do and start doing it.

Make a plan and spend your time working the plan. Stay active and continue to move forward. You've got this. When it's over, you will be stronger for the effort.

Chapter 14

BANKRUPTCY

Bankruptcy is a journey people take too lightly until they walk the journey themselves. It sounds so good to sign a court document that makes all debts disappear for a fresh new start.

That is not how it works. Bankruptcy is a big stress in your life, over and above the stress you are already facing—a stress that could cost your marriage or even your life. Before taking this step, you must weigh the benefits of bankruptcy against the stress you are already experiencing by not being able to pay your debts. It is possible the stress of your debts is greater than the stress of the bankruptcy process, making bankruptcy the preferred option.

Sometimes bankruptcy is the only way to discharge an obligation like a lease or an extreme debt when circumstances change. While it is not ideal, it is there to give people a chance to start over and there is no shame in reaching for legally prescribed options for starting over.

You will need to hire an attorney who specializes in bankruptcy to help you do this. It's ironic that you are declaring bankruptcy because you don't have any money, but you have to pay money to declare bankruptcy.

The process will include appearing before a judge and explaining why you cannot pay your debts—the very obligations you often took on willingly and contractually agreed to pay. The bankruptcy process will break many of your financial agreements.

Here are a few things to keep in mind as you consider this process:

YOU ARE NOT A FAILURE

Finding yourself in a position without the money to pay your debts does not make you a failure. In fact, it's often not even your fault. The most common reason for declaring bankruptcy is medical debt, and that is seldom planned or chosen.

SOMETIMES BANKRUPTCY IS THE ONLY OPTION

Yes, it is best to pay obligations you agreed to pay. But sometimes unforeseen circumstances prevent you from meeting your commitments. If you agreed to go on a trip with some friends and the week before you were to leave you had a stroke and couldn't walk, no one would fault you for changing your plans. Sometimes even the best plans change.

If it looks like you no longer have the resources to pay the debt, you need a new plan and bankruptcy might be that plan.

YOU WON'T LOSE EVERYTHING

Depending on your state laws, some of your assets will not be used toward paying your creditors in a bankruptcy. This could include your home, rental property, vehicles, household goods, jewelry, machinery, life insurance, and retirement accounts. It is nice to have something protected from your creditors so you don't end up on the street with only the clothes on your back. At least we no longer go to jail for being unable to pay our debts.

NOT ALL YOUR DEBTS CAN BE CANCELED

There are some types of debt a bankruptcy will not eliminate. So even if you succeed in starting over, some of your old obligations will follow you. Bankruptcy will not eliminate student loans, government debt like back taxes, or debt that was the result of fraud, child support, or alimony.

YOU WILL STILL HAVE A FINANCIAL FUTURE

When all is said and done, you may not have the "fresh start" you had hoped for. Bankruptcy will be a black cloud that will follow you for the rest of your life, but the effect fades with time. It will hurt your future prospects of borrowing money, getting a job, buying or renting a house, or starting a business. It will be a stain on your credit report for 7 to 10 years, depending on the chapter you file.

That's the downside, but there is an upside. Your actual credit score will likely go up over the next few years as your debt-to-income ratio improves and you begin paying your bills on time. If you become debt-free, many creditors will, again, want to lend you money. You will still be able to do business and most people will never know you declared bankruptcy in the past. A few years from now, life will seem normal again and the bankruptcy will only be a distant memory.

TYPES OF BANKRUPTCY

There are six different types (chapters) of bankruptcy, and the court will determine which one you use. The term *chapter* is from the specific chapter of the Bankruptcy Code where you can read the law. Two of them I will not discuss—Chapter 15, used for bankruptcies involving multiple countries, and Chapter 9, used by municipalities. The two most common types are Chapters 7 and 11.

CHAPTER 7 BANKRUPTCY (LIQUIDATION)

Chapter 7 is what you traditionally think of when you think about declaring bankruptcy and is the most common chapter used by individuals. The court will essentially sell everything you own to pay off your debts as far as the money will go. Those debts that aren't paid off when the money runs out will be eliminated and you won't need to ever pay them.

The court will only do this if they feel you won't have the ability to earn the money to pay back your debt in a reasonable time frame. If the court believes you could pay back the debt if you were given a different repayment schedule, then the court will use Chapter 13 instead.

The court will appoint a trustee to sell your assets and divvy the proceeds up amongst your creditors. This is excepting the types of debt mentioned earlier that are not wiped out in a bankruptcy.

The reality is most people who are declaring bankruptcy don't have any assets to sell. They are truly broke and considered a no-asset case.

A Chapter 7 bankruptcy will stay on your credit report for 10 years and you will not be allowed to file bankruptcy again for at least eight years.

Once people know you went bankrupt and did not pay the debts you agreed to pay, they will be more reluctant to lend you money for any reason. However in some circumstances, businesses may even work with you during the bankruptcy process.

CHAPTER 11 BANKRUPTCY (REORGANIZATION)

This is used to reorganize a business or corporation. The idea is to come up with a plan to allow the business to keep operating while meeting their debt obligations. Both the court and the creditor must agree on the plan. If the creditors think they can get their money back with the plan, they will agree. It's better to get paid over a longer period than to not get paid at all.

Chapter 11 is also used for real estate investors with a lot of property or people with super high incomes, like movie stars, big-name musicians, or pro athletes.

CHAPTER 12 BANKRUPTCY (FARMERS AND FISHERMEN)

This is a repayment plan for farmers and fishermen who need to keep their assets in order to continue their livelihood. If a farmer loses her land or a fisherman loses his boat, they have no way to make a living. The government also wants them to continue producing food for the rest of us.

CHAPTER 13 BANKRUPTCY (REPAYMENT SCHEDULE)

Chapter 7 wipes out the debt, but Chapter 13 provides a new sustainable repayment plan to keep you going while you pay off some or all of the debt. The court will come up with a re-payment plan you can handle, given your income, to pay off all of your secured debt and some of your unsecured debt.

In this case, you will be put on a court-appointed, strict budget with a Chapter 13 trustee directing your debt payments. This will stop a foreclosure and give you time to get caught up without losing your assets. It also stops the phone calls from creditors and the chaos of dealing with debts you may never be able to pay off.

The law limits the maximum amount of debt you may have in order to use Chapter 13, and this limit is updated every three years. As of April 2019, your debts must be less than $419,275 if the debt is unsecured and $1,257,850 if the debt is secured, in order to use Chapter 13. Your tax filings must also be current.

This bankruptcy will stay on your credit report for seven years and you can't file another Chapter 13 again for two years.

A BANKRUPTCY JOURNEY

Even though a bankruptcy is rough to go through, there is life after bankruptcy. You will get through it and move on with your life. Since I have never navigated through a bankruptcy myself, let's hear from someone who traveled this journey with his family and has now come out the other side. His story is one he prefers to tell anonymously.

THE RISE AND FALL OF A DREAM

One day while watching my wife homeschool our three daughters, I was thinking about how blessed we were. Because of an inheritance from my grandparents, at the time we had a mortgage-free home, no debt, and a great credit rating. My job in a manufacturing company supported us well and I began to wonder about a new dream: having my own manufacturing company.

The time was right for me to move from employee to owner and start my own company while the economy was booming. To get the seed capital for the launch, I took a 50% mortgage on my home as well as a small business loan from the government.

I rented a warehouse and built the assembly line for a product my wife's grandfather passed on to us. By the end of the summer, I was so excited to see the arrival of several pallets of custom packaging for our first Christmas season. We were about to go national and I thought Grandfather would be so proud.

Two weeks later, on September 11, 2001, I awoke to the terrible news of the terrorist attack on the World Trade Center in New York City. The nation was in shock and mourning, driving the economy to a halt. This turned out to be very bad timing for the launch of a new product. It took several years for the retail distribution system to recover.

Because of this national sales slump, my company needed new capital to stay afloat and expand distribution. It seemed the smartest move was to take on new partners to bring in the needed capital without adding more debt. Unfortunately, the cost of bringing in this new capital was the loss of control of my company. The power was shifted to those who had the "new" money to save the day. I was no longer a sole proprietor. I was now a major shareholder, but the company continued on.

By 2007, the economy was in full swing again. Housing prices were skyrocketing and investors were making a killing on real estate appreciation. Unfortunately, my little company was not making a killing, but it was hanging on.

My wife and I decided to invest in the real estate frenzy to make some of this "easy" money on the side. We purchased a beautiful, fully furnished home. It seemed too nice to become a rental and we would worry about any damage that tenants might cause that would hurt the appreciation, so we intended to leave it vacant. A few months after the new mortgage was signed, the 2008 housing crisis dropped the bottom out of the market. There would be no appreciation for a while. For the second time, our timing was thwarted by unforeseen and uncontrollable circumstances.

The crash affected sales of our manufacturing company again and my income disappeared. The next few months found us scraping for cash and we resorted to using our credit cards to cover our mortgage payments, hoping for a quick economic recovery.

The recovery didn't happen soon enough. We were now deep into our own personal financial crisis. Income from our company was gone, our investment home was in foreclosure, we were behind on the mortgage payments for our home, and our credit cards were maxed out. Over the next few months, we lost our investment house, and the home we once owned free and clear was auctioned off on the courthouse steps, purchased by the bank who held the mortgage.

Our world had been turned upside down. This was not supposed to happen to "responsible" people. From the smoking ashes of our life, we began to consider something that for us had been unthinkable: bankruptcy.

With a heavy load of shame and a feeling of foolishness and loss, we sought out a bankruptcy attorney in another town to avoid local disclosure.

Our attorney made us feel better about the situation and functioned as a cross between a counselor and a funeral director. He made us realize we were not the only family in crisis. One question he asked caught me off guard: "Is your marriage strong enough to survive this?" It seems this type of crisis takes a heavy toll on marriages and many do not survive. We thought our marriage could survive.

The next three months were humbling as we reached our lowest point in life. The court granted us full release from our debts and all future claims. We were free again and ready to start a new life, climbing our way back up from rock bottom. Yes, our marriage had been strong enough to survive this.

Two weeks after the court gave us a new start, I found a good management job and still work there today. After losing our home, we now rent a home that is nicer and costs less per month than the one we lost. We are rebuilding our credit rating, avoiding debt, and living within our means. It feels like we have our life back. The manufacturing company I started as a dream eventually closed its doors and all the invested capital was lost.

There are times I do regret what we lost. Then, I look around at my financially successful peers who have lost the important things in their pursuit of "success" and I consider myself to be truly rich. I have my wife, my daughters, my health, my God, and a clear path to an amazing future ahead of us.

I have also learned that starting a business without cash reserves is like a car without shock absorbers on a rocky road. That cash cushion can be the difference between an uncomfortable bump or a jarring event that causes a total loss of control and a fatal crash.

When struggling through a financial crisis, there are two paths available: remain within the desolation because we cannot let go of what was lost, or choose to see potential beauty in what we can become. I chose to take the new adventure.

I can now assure you there is life after bankruptcy.

Chapter 15

PROTECT YOUR MARRIAGE

(READ THIS EVEN IF YOU'RE SINGLE)

So why are we talking about marriage in a book on financial crisis? Because a financial crisis will be a great stress on your marriage. If you don't handle this carefully, you might lose your spouse. Divorce is a very expensive additional financial disaster you want to avoid. If you are married, this chapter may help you keep your relationship strong. If you are single, this chapter still has value in learning to deal with a crisis, especially if you have kids, and the next chapter addresses ways to help you weather your financial storm, mentally and emotionally.

In every study on divorce, financial issues come in high on the list of reasons that lead to a separation or divorce. Several of the couples I have coached through my financial makeover program have stated money issues are a major stress on their relationship. One couple told me they were arguing about money on a daily basis, but after a few weeks spent working on their financial problems with me, the arguments stopped.

Your financial crisis will take the stress in your marriage to a new level. If you are aware of this and deal with it in a proactive manner, you are likely to come out of this with your marriage stronger than ever. Following are a few things you can do to protect your marriage during a crisis.

COMMUNICATE

After 32 years of marriage, I have concluded that I cannot read Carolyn's mind, and she can't read mine. Yet we both still behave at times as though we can.

You must assume that if you didn't specifically tell something to your spouse, they don't know it. Since one of the reasons most people get married is to have a partner with whom you can go through the ups and downs of life, share this down in your life with your spouse. Always be truthful about the situation.

Have frequent discussions (not arguments) about your money plans. Be sure you are both working toward the same goal. Are you both willing to sell the Depression glass collection? Will you each quit putting purchases on the credit card?

Treat your household as if it were a business and hold at least a weekly business meeting during difficult times. This will help each of you stay on the same page financially. This meeting is a great time to brainstorm your options together.

NO BLAMING

It is likely no one is to blame for the situation you are in, but that is not always the case. If one spouse did something to cause the financial crisis, it is OK to acknowledge it once in the beginning, to get it off your chest, but then let it go and cast no more blame.

Your spouse didn't get up one morning and decide to make both of your lives miserable by making a financial blunder. They likely were doing what they thought was best for both of you. Once you realize this, it's easier to let go and not participate in the blame game.

Bringing up a blunder every time you talk will start a death spiral in your marriage. The blunder is in the past. To get out of this financial crisis, you must look to the future and head in that direction. It's time to forget about what got you here and work on what will get you out. Work on solutions together.

If you are responsible for the crisis, take responsibility for your actions. Own up to it, apologize, and then move on. Don't keep beating yourself up since you can't change the past. If you aren't the responsible party, give your spouse a hug and let them know you forgive them and will work with them to dig out of this situation.

KEEP THE ROMANCE ALIVE

When times get tough, there is a tendency to cut out romance. You will need to actively work on keeping the romance alive during this time just like you do the rest of the time.

Be sure you have at least one date night every week. It doesn't have to cost money. A hand-in-hand walk through the park will do wonders for your relationship. Think back to why you chose your spouse. What made them special? What drew you together? It's easy to forget your love story. It's time to remind yourself why you are together.

Find an activity you enjoy doing together. This will give you a chance to work side by side on something besides solving the crisis. Play cards, ride bikes, take walks, play doubles pickleball or some other sport, play music together, read a book together, watch a movie, or make a craft. Everyone has different interests, so you need to find one you both have in common. Togetherness is key.

When times are tough, it feels like there is nothing to appreciate. Show appreciation to your spouse. Complement them on the little things they do for the family: fixing dinner, washing the car, doing laundry, mowing the lawn, or helping the kids with their homework. Make a list of all the reasons you are thankful for your spouse.

Flirt with your spouse. You did this a lot when you were dating. Do it again now to remind them of your love. Does your spouse know you want and need them in your life? Make sure they do.

Make time for sex. Being tired and stressed is not good foreplay but it is important you stay connected in this way. Make sure your spouse knows you genuinely *want* to have sex with them, not that you are just *willing* to. They need to feel your desire for them. Don't make excuses, make love.

Keep yourself looking attractive for your spouse. When other things are on your mind, it may be easy to let your physical appearance go to pot. When I started working from home, I didn't get dressed or fix my hair in the morning. Sometimes the bathrobe look lasted all day. That's not so appealing. Even though you might not be going to work, take time for grooming in the morning.

CELEBRATE YOUR WINS

As you dig yourself out of a hole, there will be little wins along the way. Each time you reach a milestone or complete a task, have a little celebration. You might celebrate paying off a credit card, selling a large item to raise cash, completing an entire week without spending money, or anything else you are trying to accomplish.

Every time you have a celebration, you are confirming your progress. You are telling each other you're one step closer to your shared goal. It's also another thing to do together. Celebrating will help you gain momentum to attack the next goal with enthusiasm. Keep track of your progress together and you will both be anticipating the upcoming celebration.

What would be a good celebration? In advance, determine each milestone you will celebrate and decide how it will be celebrated once it is completed. Find something you both would enjoy that is very inexpensive or free. Then you also have something to look forward to.

INVOLVE THE KIDS

Your children are part of this too. Don't think they don't know what's going on. They might not know the specifics, but they know there is a problem. Give them an age-appropriate description they will understand so they will be less worried and not imagine the issues are worse than they really are.

I didn't realize how much my kids were aware of issues in our family until they were adults. Then I saw actions and heard discussions that made it clear they knew what had happened and learned from it. Make sure they hear what is happening from you so they get an accurate picture. They also need assurance that Mom and Dad's relationship is OK.

Some of your decisions might involve them. If you need to pull the kids out of private school, they need to understand the reason. They need to know it is not their fault. If they are aware of the problem, they can be part of the solution. Now they know why you can't afford to take them to McDonald's after their soccer game or tennis match like you used to. They will understand, especially if it will only be for a season, and not forever.

NEVER USE THE "D" WORD AS A WEAPON

Divorce should not be an option. If you ever bring it up as if it is an option or use it as a threat, then you are purposely driving wedges into your marriage. Don't threaten your spouse with anything. You are not enemies.

Even when the discussion gets heated, threats need to stay out of the conversation. You must create a "we are in this together to the end" attitude at all times.

Take the attitude of the military: no man left behind. Your spouse needs to know you have their back. You are with them through thick and thin. You will not bail when times get tough. This is a good time to remember your wedding vows. Maybe they sounded something like this:

"I take you to be my lawfully wedded husband/wife, forsaking all others, to have and to hold, from this day forward, for better or worse, for richer or poorer, in sickness and in health, to love and cherish through both the good times and bad times, for as long as we both shall live."

When you commit to each other, nothing can stop you—not even a little ol' financial crisis now and then.

MY STORY PART 5: THE JOB

The following Tuesday, after my unsuccessful late April job hunt on Interstate 5, the senior partner from Grants Pass called. He had spoken the day before to the doctor who was supposed to join their group. That doctor had a change of heart and decided not to join them after all. He wanted to stay at his current job.

So, the two doctors in Grants Pass did a little more checking up on this kid who fell into their laps a few days ago. The junior partner, who also trained in Bakersfield, called the chief of surgery where he and I both did our residency. After their conversation, the junior partner was very happy to move forward with a formal interview. The senior partner called Saturday evening, asking if he could fly down and spend the first Sunday in May with me to talk more in depth about the possibility of my joining their practice.

We had a great time together. He invited Carolyn and me to fly up for a formal interview the following weekend, when I would be able to meet more of the medical community. I told him I would love to, but I was on call next weekend and didn't have anyone on my team who could cover for me.

Monday morning when I walked into the surgery office, I ran into a fourth-year resident who was supposed to be on an elective rotation in another state. He told me the rotation he had been scheduled to attend was canceled, and he asked if there was anywhere I could use him. I couldn't believe my luck. I told him he could join my team and he would be on call next weekend so I could go to an interview.

Carolyn and I flew to Grants Pass that next weekend and thought this opportunity was even better than the one I had lost. I was offered the job and I accepted it on the spot. That weekend we also found a house after a three-hour search. During the last week of May, the contract was signed and I officially had a job.

Approximately seven weeks after losing the first job and thinking my life was headed for a disaster, I had a new job even better than the first one. I was on cloud nine. Looking back, I attribute this outcome to my wife's incredible support and my fast action at starting another job search. That fast action averted a potential crisis only four weeks away.

It was also fortunate the job was in the state in which I got my new license. Had I found a job in a different state where I did not have a license, there would have been a gap in my employment while I waded through the licensing process in the next state. If that had been the case, I would have needed extra funds to bridge that gap.

But then there was an unbelievable twist that happened after I started my new job.

Chapter 16

WHAT IF YOU'RE SINGLE?
(READ THIS EVEN IF YOU'RE MARRIED)

When you don't have a spouse to help carry the load, a few things are different. Coming home every day to an empty house can be hard. If you have kids, your life under normal circumstances is tough as you have no one to share the daily responsibility of raising children.

First, I hope you did not skip the last chapter simply because you aren't married. Nearly everything in the last chapter also pertains to you. So if you skipped the last chapter, go back and read it now. If you are not single, please don't skip this chapter either. Since we are all individuals, this chapter will pertain to everyone.

You, as well as those who are married, will experience the added stress in your life brought about by the crisis. So whatever relationships you do have will be stressed as well. Be sure to keep the lines of communication open with your friends. Stop any self-blame you are feeling. The downward spiral of negative thinking is even worse for those who are home alone. If you have some sort of romantic life, be sure to keep it alive through the crisis. Celebrating wins is as important for single people as it is for married couples. And if you have kids, involve them in discussing the crisis as much as you can based on their level of maturity. They can handle more than you think.

SPECIAL ISSUES

There are a few things unique to your situation. If you lose your job, the income drop for your household is 100%.

When you come home, there is no one to hold you accountable for your actions. You bear that burden alone. There is no backup person to help with the kids' needs. If your son needs to be brought home from school, you are responsible to find a way for him to get home. Second cars come in handy when mechanical issues arise, but you likely won't have that back up option.

But it's not all bad. There are some advantages to being single we must acknowledge.

ADVANTAGES OF THE SINGLE LIFE

Since you are the only one making decisions, you can act more quickly. If you want to move to a new town where a better job is available, you only need to secure one job. There is no need to search for a job for your spouse. This is a problem many couples encounter: finding a location with job opportunities for two people can be difficult.

Moving to a smaller home is much easier if you are single. You also don't need anyone else's permission or agreement.

Roommates are a much easier proposition if you are single. That opens up the opportunity to take in a boarder or move in with a friend and cut your housing costs in half instantly.

FIND A FINANCIAL FRIEND

The first thing you should do as a single person dealing with a financial crisis is find a financial friend. This person needs to be someone you trust and are comfortable sharing the details of your income and spending with. Choose someone who has their financial act together.

Give them the job of holding you accountable in the same way you would be held accountable by a spouse. If you are trying to cut back, show them evidence you have cut back.

Communicate with them regarding your finances at least once a week during the early part of the crisis. They will not only help cheer you on and encourage you to do the things you're trying to accomplish, they will also be a good sounding board and a great source of advice. If you are trying to do this by yourself, you are working with handcuffs on. Seek help.

MAINTAIN FRIENDSHIPS

Stay in contact with your friends. You need them to help relieve the stress that has crept into your life along with your crisis. When you are down, they will pick you up. A friend who makes you laugh and helps you forget the tough things in life is invaluable. It is best if they are not the same person you are baring your financial soul to, but it will be OK if they are.

While going through this tough time in your life, allow your friends to pick up your spirits and help you improve your attitude when you are down. Do fun things together that are free or inexpensive. Laughter has a way of taking away our sorrows.

PLAN AHEAD

Often in a marriage, one person is the planner and the other follows. In your case, no matter what your natural tendency is, you need to be the planner and the follower. Don't run the risk of coming home after a long day and sitting in front of the TV the rest of the night. Make plans that will get you out of this crisis and follow them.

If you were not planning before this happened, now is the time to start. Going through the process of making a budget is a good start. Follow through with the plans you make, even though no one is watching.

AVOID IMPULSE BUYING

With no one at home to hold you accountable for your spending, it is easy to buy something as a pick-me-up. No one else will ask why you made a particular purchase. Did you really need those shoes? Is your old drill all that bad?

Impulse buying is a huge hit to your spending plan and you are the only one who can stop it from happening. When I was a resident, one of my fellow residents was always complaining about his horrible student debt burden. It was depressing him. One day he drove into the parking lot in a brand-new sports car. I asked him how he could afford such a car with so much debt. He told me he needed a pick-me-up, so he bought a new car. I doubt his elation continued past the first car payment.

NO NEGATIVE SELF-TALK

Negative head games are especially bad if you come home to an empty house. There is no one to distract your thinking. Blaming yourself is OK the first time you do it, if your actions truly caused the crisis—it is good to realize that your actions have consequences. Then forgive yourself and move on. To continue beating yourself up for past mistakes will not get you to a better future.

GET YOUR LEGAL AFFAIRS IN ORDER

There are three legal items single people tend to postpone.

MAKE A WILL

If you were to die, what would become of your estate? Who would be in charge of your children? These are questions you do not want the state or a court to decide. You will have more peace of mind knowing these things are covered.

HEALTHCARE POWER OF ATTORNEY

Who will speak for you if you can't? If you are hospitalized and put on a ventilator, who will make your medical decisions? Your physicians need to know the answer to this question. Assign someone you trust to act in your best interest. Then tell them what your wishes are so they can truly speak for you.

DURABLE POWER OF ATTORNEY

If you become sick or injured and are laid up for a few months, you need someone to be able to run your affairs. Who will pay the bills? You don't want to return home only to find you lost your house while you were in the hospital recovering.

Be sure this person knows where to find your important documents and has access to your house.

STAND UP FOR YOURSELF

You are your only advocate. If you are having financial difficulty, tell your friends why you can't go out for lunch. There is a lot of social pressure when friends get together. Don't let that be the driving force in your life. Stand up for yourself and be heard. If they know what is happening, they might even help.

There is no one but you to take action during the golden week. Do what is necessary to get what you need. Don't forget to be proud of yourself for all you have accomplished.

Never forget the words of my brother, Ron Fawcett:

"The true heroes in the world are single parents."

Chapter 17

WHEN YOUR JOB IS YOUR IDENTITY

One of the biggest issues many professionals face is having their identity tied to their career. If that's you, when your career goes, your identity is in danger of going with it.

I spent many years working toward achieving the title of doctor, then even more years to complete my training. Thirteen years after high school, I could finally begin practicing as a surgeon. What would happen if I couldn't find work in my chosen career? What if I got injured and couldn't work? What if I lost my state license or my hospital admitting privileges?

For some professions, the person's career is referenced when they are being addressed by other people. Let me introduce to you Astronaut Neil Armstrong, President Ronald Reagan, Governor Andrew Cuomo, Reverend Billy Graham, Admiral Halsey, and Doctor Cory Fawcett. These careers are part of our identity.

If I lose my ability to work, by losing my license for example, I lose part of my identity. If your financial crisis involves the loss of your job as well as your identity, that is a double whammy.

But you are not only a doctor, attorney, pastor, or governor. You are also a husband/wife, father/mother, friend, son/daughter, and community member. You are still you. You still have the skills and talents you always had. That will never change, even if you lose your career.

Before I retired from medicine, I wondered if I would miss being a surgeon. Turns out I did not miss medicine. I also did not lose my identity, and neither will you if you can't work in your career any longer.

LOSS OF LICENSE

One of the most frustrating things about being a professional is the need for a state license. A state board made up of people who don't know you determines if you are fit to do your job. Any problem you have can result in you losing your license. Sometimes it is only perceived problems that raise the flag.

These boards have ultimate power over your ability to work. If they decide not to give you a license in their state or revoke the license you have, then you don't work. If they tell you to do something to get your license back, you have no choice but to do what they say. Sometimes you feel helpless to control your destiny.

But you are not helpless. You still have options. You can get a state license somewhere else, contest the decision, or move on to another career that builds on what you already know. Your skills do not vanish by any action a board might take. They do not hold your identity in the palm of their hands.

LOSS OF CONTROL

During the coronavirus pandemic and national shutdown, all elective medical procedures were halted. This was a case when totally functioning businesses were suddenly shut down without warning and told to stay that way until further notice. This occurred through no fault of the doctors.

There have been many psychological studies over the years showing a correlation between mental health and control of your environment. For many professionals, this loss of control is new to them and potentially harmful. Don't sit back passively and sulk over your loss. Find the things you can control and control them. You can still see patients in need and schedule their procedure for later, set up a telehealth business to help your patients, or volunteer your services in the hospital. Losing control over one thing is not losing control over everything.

THREAT OF LITIGATION

Physicians especially are under constant threat of litigation. For some, this can be paralyzing, especially when an error was truly made in regard to a patient. If the physician is found guilty of negligence, it could lead to a financial crisis if he or she is found to be liable for more than their malpractice insurance covers. Likewise, if the incident leads to the loss of privileges, it will have a huge economic impact.

When a physician is sued by a patient, it is a direct assault on their ability to do their job—which is a direct assault on their identity. They must disconnect the patient's attempt to obtain monetary compensation from the notion that they are not fit for the job.

If you are a physician, you will likely get sued as it is a common occurrence, but you must not take it personally.

LOSS OF REPUTATION

Many professionals are well known in the community. If they have a financial crisis, they may find themselves in the local newspaper. Soon much of the town knows of their problems and their difficulties are no longer private.

Losing a good reputation will have an effect on your identity.

WHAT IF YOU CAN NEVER DO YOUR PROFESSION AGAIN?

Sometimes a financial crisis is caused by a career-ending event. Yet you still retain the knowledge you have gained in your training and experience. Other people might be interested in building on that outside the confines of your lost career.

My book *The Doctors Guide to Smart Career Alternatives and Retirement* covers many different avenues physicians can take using their degree without doing clinical work. Starting over in a completely different field might be necessary, but first consider jobs that can use the skills and training you already have.

As an example, a physician who has a great interest in computer technology can work for a software company that develops products for hospitals or physician's offices. The physician has the inside scoop on what is needed. An airline pilot who can no longer fly could teach ground school. Think about what other skills you have that can combine with your training and think outside the box for new career possibilities.

FINDING A NEW IDENTITY

Sometimes a crisis is so devastating that your total identity is lost, and you can no longer perform your prior occupation. This is when a clean start in some other field is needed. The following story is an example of an attorney whose career came to an abrupt halt. If he found his identity in being an attorney, who would he be now?

AN ATTORNEY NO MORE

Some careers blur the line between the person and their job. As an attorney, my identity was tied to the job that I loved. I had a wife, four wonderful kids, and a thriving law practice. I was involved in local charitable organizations and had a good standing in my community.

Then one day I started down the proverbial slippery slope of marginal dealings. Things snowballed and I eventually crossed the legal line. I knew I was in trouble long before the FBI came knocking on my office door. But once I crossed the line, I felt paralyzed, helplessly waiting to get caught. I hope you never find yourself in such a position. In my case, the troubles that came down on me were of my own doing.

I was eventually convicted of my crimes, sentenced to time in federal prison, and ordered to pay restitution to the tune of seven figures. As the heavy metal door slammed shut on my cell, it also slammed shut on everything in my life.

I lost my career when I was disbarred, my wife sought a divorce, two of my four children rejected and disowned me and haven't spoken to me since, some of my brothers and sisters no longer speak to me, and my standing in the community I was so involved with fell to total disdain, if you can believe the newspapers. My life as I knew it was totally destroyed.

Who was I now? With a criminal record and no way to practice law, how would I ever be able to earn the money to pay seven figures of restitution? I would never again reach the financial comfort and security I once had. I thought, "If I'm going to lose everything anyway, why not make a run for it and start over somewhere new, where no one knows me? Will anyone ever want me to be their friend or lover again? Will anyone ever trust me again?"

It was so easy to beat myself up and keep reminding myself how stupid I was. One of the first things I needed to do was forgive myself. I believe this was the first step to my recovery. *Total Forgiveness: When Everything in You Wants to Hold a Grudge, Point a Finger, and Remember the Pain—God Wants You to Lay It All Aside* by R.T. Kendall (Charisma House, revised edition, 2007) was one of the first books I read in prison. His message is this: we are all human, we all make mistakes, we all sin, and we all need to forgive ourselves.

I am so thankful for the friends who helped me along the way and never abandoned me for making a mistake. One gave me an interim job for three years during the investigation, another took over the responsibility of closing my law practice, one asked me if I was suicidal, my doctor gave me anti-anxiety medication to help me function, my church paid for a counselor to help me through the emotional trauma, and most of all, my mom stood by me and provided love and support. I don't know how I could have done it without the help of these heroes.

After serving my time, I left prison. Having lost everything, my identity as an attorney was gone. I literally started my life over. Before my sentencing, my attorney told me my life would be different in the future, but it would still be good. Turned out he was right.

Time healed some relationships while I formed other new meaningful ones. I did find love again and have remarried. I have a good life today, but it is very different from the life I envisioned when I started my law practice. My retirement years will definitely be affected.

What have I learned from all this?

✓ My true identity is found in Christ, not in my career. (I was a Christian before the slippery slope began.)

✓ No matter how bad things get, tomorrow is a new day.

✓ Don't beat yourself up for your mistakes.

✓ When you think you are in trouble, seek help early.

✓ No matter how bad it gets, some friends will stand by you.

✓ Keep in mind the things that are truly important.

✓ There is life after a total financial/life catastrophe.

Chapter 18

RECOVERY

Every crisis comes to an end and yours will too. Once you are no longer in survival mode, it's time to begin getting your life back to normal. Several things might still be out of whack. You may have canceled some things you would like to add back into your life. You might be behind on some payments you made special arrangements for, and your emergency fund might be running on empty.

REASSESS

Go back and reread chapter 2 on assessing the situation and reassess where you are now. You need to know your exact new starting point before you can begin putting your finances back in order. Continue living on your reduced monthly budget while implementing what you will learn in this chapter. If you keep your expenses low and don't immediately jump back to your pre-crisis spending, you will be able to recover much faster. The following steps will get your household fully recovered and ready for the next crisis before it arrives.

MAKE A RECOVERY BUDGET

What are your new goals? Getting out of debt, refilling the emergency fund, getting back on track for retirement?

You might find that after going through a crisis, you have different goals than before. Some of the things you thought were important before may not have the same importance now. If your kids have been in public school for a while for the first time, you can now compare public and private from your first-hand experience. What is your school choice now?

This is another great time in life when a spending plan is crucial. You are making a change and you want to know exactly how much money you can allocate to each category to meet your new goals. Use the budget form in chapter 3.

Incorporate your new goals into your plan. Then stick to this new budget until your goals have been met. Don't let off the gas because things are going well. There could be another crisis someday, and you want to be better prepared than you were this time.

If you do not have enough money to accomplish all your goals at once with your new budget, prioritize them and work on each in order. This is my recommended order:

1. Catch up on delinquent bills.

2. Replenish the emergency fund to at least one month of your new living expenses.

3. Restart retirement contributions up to the employer match.

4. Begin the process of getting out of debt using the snowball method.

5. Begin moving your emergency fund up to six months' living expenses.

6. Restart full retirement plan contributions.

REFILL THE EMERGENCY FUND

Most people who actually go through a financial crisis are very appreciative of having money in the bank. Having lived through a crisis, you can now get a good handle on the amount of emergency funding that is right for you and your spending habits. Would your life have been better if you had a larger emergency fund? If so, how much money do you wish you had available for this emergency?

Set an amount for your emergency fund and pick a target date by which you will have the fund replenished. You will not be able to do this in a month, so set a reasonable goal. If you keep your spending down during the recovery time, you should be able to have the fund replaced within three years. But make your first priority to get it back up to one month's expenses right away.

If you feel you need $50,000 in the fund and you want it up to that level three years from now, you will need to put $1,389 per month back into that account ($50,000/36). If that's too much per month, then you will need to adjust the target or lengthen the time to get there.

If you are one of the people who previously decided you didn't need an emergency fund and would instead use either your investments or your borrowing power in an emergency, how did that work out? Is there anything you would adjust about that plan? Did it involve borrowing money you now need to pay back with interest? Are you OK with that?

ELIMINATE DEBT

If you went into this crisis with a lot of debt, how did that turn out? What would it have been like if you had started with no debt? Which would you have preferred?

Frankly, if you are living within your income, have a large emergency fund, and no debt, it's pretty hard to get into too much financial trouble. So, let's make a plan to get out of debt so the next time a crisis hits, you will enter it without the obligation of debt repayment.

Start by reading my book *The Doctors Guide to Eliminating Debt*. Then use the snowball method to pay back the debt by listing your debts from smallest outstanding balance to largest outstanding balance. Figure out how much money your budget can handle to put toward paying off the debt ahead of schedule. Then make the minimum payments to every debt except the smallest.

Add the money you have determined you can use for debt elimination to each monthly payment of the smallest debt. That debt will be paid off quite rapidly. Then roll all the money that had been going to the smallest debt into the payment of the next smallest debt on the list, including the minimum payment you were making on the first debt you repaid. As you pay off each debt, roll the payments into the next debt payment.

In most cases, you will have all your debts paid off except the home mortgage in two to three years. Then you can tackle that last biggest debt, which will take five to seven more years to pay off. When that is gone, you will not be at risk of losing your house to foreclosure in the next crisis.

A note on credit card debt: It is very hard to get a credit card paid off if you are still using it. The extra money you pay is going toward the money you spent the current month first, before paying off the old balance. If you need to use a credit card, use one with no outstanding balance and pay it in full every month.

REEVALUATE YOUR INVESTMENT ALLOCATION

Before this crisis, you may have had an investment allocation for stocks, bonds, cash, and whatever else you invested in. How did you feel about that allocation during the crisis? If the stock market crashed and you panicked and started selling, then you need to change your allocation to something you can be at peace with during a market crash.

If you did not feel good about the drop in the stock market, then you need to shift more money into bonds and cash. Look back at the situation you lived through and ask yourself what you wish your investment allocation looked like before the crash started. Whatever the answer is, that is how you should rebalance your investment portfolio now.

Position yourself so you will not panic during the next stock market drop. You know there will be one. They happen frequently and it is a totally normal part of the investment cycle. You need to find your happy place—the allocation that will let you sleep at night during a crash or a long bear market. That is the allocation you must find for yourself.

You don't need to make the change all at once. If you had 100% of your portfolio invested in stock before your crisis and now you prefer an investment ratio of 50% stock and 50% bonds, simply put all new money you invest into bonds until you reach the 50:50 point. Or you could sell any stock you no longer wish to own and convert that money to bonds. Set a target date to have your portfolio investments changed to your desired ratio and gradually make the changes needed to get there.

REEVALUATE YOUR RETIREMENT PLANS

If you were near retirement, this crisis might have been a big setback to those plans. How big is the setback? With your new budget and retirement contributions, what is your new target date for retirement?

You might need to work a little longer and wait for a higher social security payment before retiring. Every year you wait is another 8% in your social security paycheck. Every year you work is another year's worth of retirement plan contributions to beef up those accounts. It is also another year before you start withdrawing money from the account.

If you now have $1,000,000 in your retirement plan, the 4% rule would mean you could safely take out $40,000 a year to live on when you retire. If your money is growing at an average of 6% a year and you put $19,500 into the plan each year, then waiting for three more years would allow the account to grow to $1,256,821. The 4% rule would then let you take out $50,273 a year, which is a $10,273 per year increase.

If you would receive a $36,000 per year ($3,000 per month) social security payment if you retired right now, then an 8% a year increase would give you about $45,349 a year ($3,779 per month) if you postponed by three years. That is a $9,349 per year increase in your social security check.

Putting the two together, working three more years increases your retirement income from $76,000 a year to $95,622 a year. That is $19,622 more a year for the rest of your life.

Calculate how much longer you will need to work to reach the retirement income you desire. I suspect that having lived through a financial crisis, you might increase your retirement income target from its previous level.

GET YOUR LEGAL HOUSE IN ORDER

I discussed this in chapter 16 but will reiterate it here. Be sure you have an up-to-date will, healthcare power of attorney, and durable power of attorney in place. Now that you have lived through a crisis, you may be more attuned to their importance.

BEING PREPARED MAKES ALL THE DIFFERENCE

Preparation is everything when it comes to dealing with a crisis. The more you have prepared before the crisis hits, the better you will be able to weather the storm. Imagine the different outcomes of the following two imaginary people when a hurricane strikes their neighborhood.

PREPAREDNESS IS PERSONAL

Peter Prepared is a stickler for being ready for anything. He loves the ocean and wanted to build a house on the beach. He checked out the area and realized it lies in the hurricane belt and gets hit, on average, every other decade. Peter doesn't want to lose his house to a hurricane.

He carefully selects a firm, rocky area to pour the foundation of his house. The local building codes require special reinforcements in the house to support it in high winds. Peter asked the contractor to double the supports required. Because much of the damage to a house during a hurricane is from high water, he put all the important areas of the house on the upper floor.

Nigel Normal also loves to hang out at the beach. He wants to be as close to the water as possible. There was a lovely spot down near the water that Peter had rejected because he thought the ground wasn't firm enough to build. Nigel didn't think it was all that bad and he wanted to be able to walk right out and into the waves. Since the city had approved this lot, it must be OK.

Wanting to save a little money on the house, Nigel built it according to code but didn't put in any extras. He didn't want to waste money on extra reinforcement for the house, since hurricanes don't happen very often and he felt the standards were "standard" for a reason.

One day, a hurricane started heading toward their beach. Both Peter and Nigel followed the orders to evacuate the area to get out of harm's way. Peter secured the window shutters he had specially designed to protect against the wind and went to his mother's house to wait out the storm. Nigel put large plywood boards over the doors and windows and grabbed a couple of things that were very important to him before heading inland out of danger.

A week later, they both came back to the beach and what do you suspect they found? Peter's house had a little damage to one corner of the roof and an outside staircase was missing. His extra efforts paid off. Nigel could find no evidence his house ever existed. He learned that following the norm would not stop the damage of a hurricane.

Proper financial preparation may seem painful and more costly at the outset, but in the long run it can prevent you from losing everything when disaster strikes. If you are like Nigel Normal today, then tomorrow you can be like Peter Prepared. Next time a storm hits your life, you will be prepared.

If you do the things I covered in this chapter, you will be better prepared for the next crisis to hit. Was there something else you discovered during this crisis that you feel should be changed about your life? If so, get started on making those changes.

Chapter 19

LEAN ON YOUR FAITH

LEARN TO BE CONTENT

America is home to many people who believe in God. Our national motto is "In God We Trust." We need to remember that just because we believe doesn't mean there won't be hard times. Bad things happen to good people and good things happen to bad people. That's just the way it is.

What's important is how we react to the bad things that happen to us. Do we continue to trust God even in the tough times, or are we fair-weather Christians? Jesus and all His disciples lived through some pretty tough times. Most of them died a violent death, even though they were considered to be good people.

If we look at the Apostle Paul, he had quite the rollercoaster life. First, he was very high up in the Jewish religious order—a wealthy and powerful man who oversaw the killing of many

Christians. Then he met Jesus and converted to Christianity. He lost everything from his former life and started over to become one of the most influential Christians in history. Paul had this to say in Philippians 4:11-13 (NIV):

> "I am not saying this because I am in need, for I have learned to be content whatever the circumstances. I know what it is to be in need, and I know what it is to have plenty. I have learned the secret of being content in any and every situation, whether well fed or hungry, whether living in plenty or in want. I can do all this through him who gives me strength."

Paul **learned** to be content, regardless of the circumstances. Contentment is a choice and can be learned. That is the choice you need to make when facing a crisis. Choose to be content and enjoy life in all circumstances.

DON'T BE GRIPPED BY WORRY

If we can learn to be content in every situation, then we can stop worrying about the situation. Jesus had this to say in Matthew 6:27 (NIV):

"Can any one of you by worrying add a single hour to your life?"

In fact, coming from the point of view of a physician, I can tell you worry will actually take time away from your life. Worry and stress are far more likely to shorten lives! And worry doesn't actually fix any problems—only action will.

REJOICE AND DON'T GIVE UP HOPE

When you look back at this crisis, you will probably not remember all the pain, anguish, and despair you felt at the time. You are more likely to remember the good things that resulted from your temporary troubles.

We should be rejoicing in our lives through both the good and the bad times. Life is good. Even the times of suffering will have good points to find. Romans 5:3-4 (NIV) says this:

. . . but we also glory in our sufferings, because we know that suffering produces perseverance; perseverance, character; and character, hope.

There is always hope. When you have hope, you can do whatever it takes.

GAIN WISDOM

King Solomon is thought to be the wisest man to ever live. Fortunately for us, he recorded his wisdom for us to read. It is the book of Proverbs in the old testament of the Bible. These words of wisdom are spread out over 31 chapters, one for every day of the month. If you were to read one chapter every day for a month, you would pick up great pearls of wisdom.

Whether or not you are a believer in God, the wisdom is still valid and useful. Each time you read Proverbs, you will learn something new. Proverbs 2:10 (NIV) states this:

> For wisdom will enter your heart, and knowledge will be pleasant to your soul.

TAKE ACTION: THE NEXT RIGHT THING

So what action should you take? Do the next right thing. Then the next. And another one after that. Keep doing the next right thing until you reach your objective.

Remember the old children's story of the tortoise and the hare? That tortoise just kept on going with his goal in mind, just like you should. King Solomon had this to say in Proverbs 21:5 (NIV):

> The plans of the diligent lead to profit as surely as haste leads to poverty.

I would recommend you follow his advice. Diligently make plans and carry them out. Over time you will reach your objectives.

Don't lose your faith. You don't have any idea what tomorrow will bring, so live today to its fullest and may God bless you.

MY STORY PART 6: A MIRACLE?

During the summer after our move, Carolyn and I were thinking about all the little things that came together for me to end up in what turned out to be my dream job. Although I only mentioned a few of them in my story, there were so many that we decided to write them down. Some of them even predated my job search. We recorded 20 different "coincidences" that each could have pushed us down a different road if they hadn't happened—and I would likely not have ended up living in Grants Pass, Oregon.

After I had been working for a few weeks and we had gotten to know more people in town, we learned some interesting information. While we had been praying for the right job to come along and our friends and family had also been praying for us, what we didn't know at the time of our interview was several people in Grants Pass were praying that the surgeon my partners had originally chosen would not take the job. Several people in our church (the same church my senior partner attended) did not have a good feeling about the surgeon who was coming. So, they prayed for a different surgeon to come along to fill that spot. I turned out to be the one to fill the position.

A few weeks after I started seeing patients, a new patient came in for a consult. After completing the consult, he told me something that stopped me in my tracks. He said the real reason he came was to give me a message from God.

When someone tells you they have a message from God, it gets your attention. That doesn't happen every day, and has never happened to me before or since, so he definitely had my attention. He said God wanted me to know that He was the one who sent me to Grants Pass because there was something He wanted me to do here. This man didn't know what I was supposed to do. He was just delivering the message as instructed. He also wanted me to know that I was the answer to many people's prayers. He then thanked me for the consult and left.

I sat in the chair with goose bumps, while I replayed in my head what had just happened. A string of 20 "coincidences" fell into place for me to get what turned out to be my dream job. Then this man comes to me with a message from God, implying those events were not coincidences! Now I wondered why I was brought to Grants Pass.

There were many things I was part of during my 27 years living in Grants Pass that could have been the reason, but I never figured out exactly why God brought me to the town where I have lived most of my adult life. Maybe His reason for bringing me here hasn't happened yet.

Even though losing my initial job only three months before finishing my residency seemed like a disaster to me at the time, it turned out to be a blessing in disguise. Life is like that. There will always be good times and bad times, ups and downs, despair and joy, but in the end, things seem to work out. Through this journey, I could clearly see how one door closed and another opened.

Looking back, this Bible verse, Romans 8:28 (NIV), comes to mind:

> **And we know that in all things God works for the good of those who love him, who have been called according to his purpose.**

Incidentally, I later met the surgeon who was hired for that first job instead of me. It was about seven years after residency, and he was in the process of looking for a new job. It turned out not to be a great place to work. He told me I was fortunate to have not been chosen for the job.

Today the feelings from that tough time have long been forgotten. Compared to what you may be going through now, it likely doesn't even seem like much of a tough time. Remember what I said about a minor surgery being one that is performed on someone else. But those feelings of despair were real for me at the time. Time heals all wounds.

ACKNOWLEDGMENTS

No one writes a good book alone. They have a lot of help. This book was especially trying as I set a very aggressive goal of moving from idea to published in one month. If you have ever written a book, you know what I'm talking about. Consequently, I need to thank my wife, Carolyn, for putting up with a horrendous schedule of fierce writing. On the bright side, it did give us something productive to do when we were isolated during the pandemic. She also went above the call of duty and followed behind me editing the chapters as I wrote them.

A special thanks to those who did the test reading of this book and offered suggested improvements: Ashvin K. Amara, M.D., Natalie Doyle, M.D., Steven J. Engman, M.D., Ph.D., Karen Haslund, M.D., Joan Hill, Bradley P. Meyer, M.D., David Reyes, M.D., MPH, Joseph Russell, M.D., Alex Sadauskas, M.D., Nathan Shumway, D.O., FACP, Sasha Taylor, Marc Warner, M.D., and Jeff Wiencek, M.D.

Three people were kind enough to speak to me about the special considerations of being single. It has been so long since I was single, it's hard to remember what that was like. So thanks to Ron Fawcett, Debbie Lindley, and Cali Wright.

Then there are the three who were willing to share their own troubled times with us: Dr. Christopher Yerington and our two anonymous contributors. Thank you for baring your souls and giving us all hope, knowing there is life after a crisis.

There are many others along the way who contributed to the information I've learned through the years and that I am now passing on to you. I'm sorry I can't list them all, or even remember them all, as they are too numerous to count.

I am ever thankful for those who continue to buy and read the books and online courses in the *Doctors Guide* series. You make me want to write more. Thanks for your support.

Thanks to the team at Aloha Publishing, including Maryanna Young and Jennifer Regner, and the Fusion Creative Works design team of Shiloh Schroeder, Rachel Langaker, and Jessi Carpenter. Without them, this book would still be just an idea floating around in my mind.

ABOUT THE AUTHOR

Dr. Cory S. Fawcett's passion for teaching personal finance spans his entire career. Through one-on-one counseling as a Crown Financial Ministries small group discussion leader (a 10-week Bible study on money management) and as a keynote speaker, he has been improving people's financial and professional lives for years. As an instructor for medical students and residents, he found they have a hunger and need for financial wisdom and direction as they transform into practicing physicians. He is the author of *The Doctors Guide* book series, all of which have become best sellers and many have received awards, including *The Doctors Guide to Starting Your Practice/Career Right*, *The Doctors Guide to Eliminating Debt*, *The Doctors Guide to Smart Career Alternatives and Retirement,* and *The Doctors Guide to Real Estate Investing for Busy Professionals.*

With his financial interest and background knowledge, he has served on several boards and financial committees throughout the years. He has been involved as an owner, founder, or partner in more than two dozen business and real estate ventures.

His current mission is teaching doctors to have healthy, happy, and debt-free lives—to regain control of their practices, their time, and their finances. He is writing, speaking, and coaching in an effort to improve the lives of his colleagues. Burnout, suicide, debt, and bankruptcy are increasing among physicians, dentists, optometrists, chiropractors, pharmacists, nurse practitioners, and others in the healthcare industry, and he focuses on halting the progression of these unnecessary outcomes.

Dr. Fawcett is an award-winning and best-selling author, keynote speaker, entrepreneur, and a repurposed general surgeon. He completed his bachelor's degree in biology at Stanford University, his Doctor of Medicine at Oregon Health and Science University, and his general surgery residency at Kern Medical Center. After completing his training, he returned to southern Oregon to practice for 20 years in a single-specialty private practice group in Grants Pass. Then for three years, he worked part time in rural hospitals, providing call coverage before devoting his time to helping healthcare professionals thrive.

Since 1988, he has shared his home with his lovely bride, Carolyn. They have two boys: Brian, who graduated from college with a degree in economics, and Keith, who graduated with a degree in mobile development.

ABOUT *THE DOCTORS GUIDE* SERIES

The Doctors Guide series aims to improve the lives of doctors on both a personal and a financial level and includes the following:

The Doctors Guide to Starting Your Practice/Career Right

Every resident should read this book as they start their final year of training. I wish it would be given out in every residency program. If that would happen, the state of medicine in America would be greatly improved.

This is the book that will help the resident doctor make a smooth and successful transition into the life of an attending. Whether as a business owner or an employed physician, there are so many things to consider. This book will pave the way to success.

The Doctors Guide to Eliminating Debt

Debt has become a terrible burden for many of my colleagues. It's not just the debt they accumulate during their training. Once that attending income begins to roll in, everyone wants to lend the new doctor some money. The tendency to take those loans has put many a doctor into financial bondage.

It is time we all stop managing our debt and start eliminating it. We must work hard to eliminate Debtabetic Neuropathy and Alzheimer's Debtmentia in our lifetime. Lifelong debt is not the best path.

The Doctors Guide to Smart Career Alternatives and Retirement

Many physicians are hurting today and feel betrayed by their profession. They are ready to leave medicine after all those years to get here. There are alternatives to this path. This book walks you through three options: Changes you can make to enjoy your practice more, new career alternatives for physicians that build on your vast knowledge, and if neither of those will work, then it becomes a how-to guide to wind down a practice and retire.

The Doctors Guide to Real Estate Investing for Busy Professionals

Many busy professionals think they don't have enough time to invest in real estate. They have the mistaken notion that it takes more time than they have. When other physicians found out I managed 64 apartment units, they were always surprised. "How can you possibly have time for that?" was the most common question. In this book, I show you exactly how you can have time to invest in real estate even if you are a busy professional.

The Doctors Guide to Thriving in Locum Tenens

This online video course includes everything you need to know to thrive in locum tenens. Many doctors are thinking about locums but are not sure how to start. I spent three years doing locum tenens and put all the information I learned into this course so you don't have to reinvent the wheel. Whether you want to do locums full time, part time, or just one weekend a month, this course will help you be successful.

QUESTIONS? COMMENTS?

Dr. Cory S. Fawcett
FinancialSuccessMD.com

I wrote this book to share what I have learned over the years about dealing with difficult times. There are definite action steps you can take to get through a financial crisis and become better prepared for the next one. I also want to hear about your experiences. Any feedback is welcome, and I want to know if you think I've missed an important topic, you have a story to tell, or you found a mistake. Also, I didn't put everything I know into this book. Send me an email at md@financialsuccessmd.com or contact me through my website at FinancialSuccessMD.com.

If you found this book to be useful, please post a review on Amazon, spread the word in social media, and pass on what you have learned to your colleagues.

Connect with Financial Success MD on LinkedIn

Like @FinancialSuccessMD on Facebook

Follow @Fin_SuccessMD on Twitter

Email md@financialsuccessmd.com

Watch Financial Success MD on YouTube

Follow my blog at FinancialSuccessMD.com

Join me at financialsuccessmd on Instagram

Pin me at financialsuccessmd on Pinterest